A MAN FOR GOD
AND FOR OTHERS
A Personal Reflection on Catholic Priesthood

By

Rev. Fr. F. Igwenwanne, Ph.D. BCC

Fr. Fidelis Igwenwanne
Pastoral Centre
P.O. Box 63
Issele – UKU
Delta State, Nigeria

Nihil Obstat
Rev. Michael L. Diskin
Assistant Chancellor
Diocese of Phoenix
400 E. Monroe Street
Phoenix, AZ 85004-2336
June 26, 2012

Imprimatur
Most Rev. Thomas J. Olmsted
Bishop of Phoenix
Diocesan Pastoral Center
400 E. Monroe Street
Phoenix, AZ 85004-2336
June 26, 2012

ISBN 978-2919-85-3

PRINTED BY **BUSINESS CATCHERS FOR YOU**
2985 W. Osborn Road, Phoenix, Arizona 85017
Phone: (602) 252-5687 • www.bc4u.com

DISTRIBUTED BY CHRIST THE KING PARISH GIFT SHOP
1551 E Dana Ave., Mesa, Arizona 85204-1200
For additional copies please contact:
Mendy bayda (480) 964-1719, Email: mbayda@ctk-catholic.org
or visit parish website: www.ctk-catholicschool.org

ACKNOWLEDGEMENT

One of the turning points in my priestly life took place when I preached a diocesan annual retreat for the Bishop and priests of the Diocese of Ahiara in Nigeria. In attendance were well over 120 priests. There and then, I felt called and inspired to a deeper reflection on the Catholic priesthood and its relationship to People of God and the world. Committing this reflection to writing in the form of a book was like a dream realized.

The writing of this book took a lot of energy and determination; I wouldn't have succeeded without support from people, including family and friends. These deserve some acknowledgements:

First and foremost, all glory and honor belongs to God for the wisdom, intelligence and energy to embark on this work. Thanks to Mother Mary, Mother of all priests

I thank the Bishop and the diocesan priests of Ahiara whose interactions, attentiveness, thought-provoking questions and comments spurred me to forge ahead in the production of this work. As a matter of fact, they encouraged me to publish this work. The preparation for this retreat challenged me to make an in depth spiritual reflection and further my research on priestly holiness. So this book is basically the by-product of the materials for this retreat. Furthermore, I wish to acknowledge that this retreat largely depended on the materials of the worldwide retreat for priests held in Rome.

There is a legend once told by Henry Wadsworth Longfellow, about the boy who gave up his five barley loaves and two small fishes so that Christ could feed the multitude. It tells how the boy hurried home, after all the fragments had been gathered and told his mother about the exciting incident. With eyes still big with wonder, he told her how his five little barley cakes and two dried fishes had multiplied in the Savior's hand until there was enough to satisfy 5,000 hungry people. This boils down to the fact that no one is kind to only one person, but to many persons, through one.

In the light of the above fact, I wish to acknowledge that this revised edition, which many people now enjoy across the globe, wouldn't have been possible without the wonderful people of the Diocese of Phoenix, Arizona, in the United States of America. Their support and encouragement motivated me to write this revised edition when the second edition ran out of stock.

I thank Most Rev. Thomas O'Brien, the emeritus Bishop of the Diocese of Phoenix, for inviting me to this great diocese. Thanks also to Fr. Tom Zurcher CSC, the former vicar for priests, for welcoming me and supporting me. Going from Nigeria to Rome and moving from Rome to the USA was like coming into the hues of many colors; Fr. Tom's warm *persona* was all I needed to know that I was in the right place at the right time.

My special thanks goes to Most Rev. Thomas Olmsted, the Bishop of the Diocese of Phoenix, for his fatherly support to my priestly ministry here and for giving the imprimatur to this book. My appreciation goes also to the Auxiliary Bishop of this Diocese, Most Rev. Eduardo Nevares, for all his goodness and support to me. I would also like to thank Most Rev. Jim Wall, former vicar for Priests for the Diocese of Phoenix, and now the Bishop of Gallup. I have great respect for these Bishops, and I see them as great men with pastoral hearts of love for their people.

My profound gratitude also goes to Rev. David Sanfillipo, our Vicar for Priests, for his wonderful support to my ministry in the Diocese of Phoenix. As a wonderful vicar, he listens and takes special interest in our concerns and individual issues. Special thanks to Rev. Michael Diskin, the Vice Chancellor of the Diocese of Phoenix for his painstaking effort reviewing this book and giving Nihil Obstat to it.

I will not forget to thank all the priests of the Diocese of Phoenix for their fraternal support: the first name that comes to mind is Rev. Michael Deptula, the first priest I worked with in Lake Havasu City, and his successor, Rev. Chauncey Winkler, the current pastor of Our Lady of the Lake Catholic Church, Lake Havasu City. Other priests who deserve special thanks are: Rev. Richard Felt, Rev. Steven Kunkel (who wrote the foreword to this book), Rev. Peter Bui, Rev. Thomas Hallsten, Rev. Mike Ashibuogwu, Rev. Sylvester Modebei, Rev. Paul Sullivan, Msgr. George Highberger, Rev. Matthews Munjanath, Rev. Peter Rossa and Rev. Craig Friedley, etc., for their fraternal collaboration in priestly ministry.

As the saying goes, "any river that forgets its source runs dry." On this note, I would like to thank the great people of Lake Havasu City, my first stop in the United states of America. I will never forget Lake Havasu City. My priestly ministry in Our Lady of the Lake Parish, where I was a Parochial Vicar for five years, touched my heart more than anything else ever did in my life. The job of a priest is to tend to the spiritual needs of people. Living in Lake Havasu City taught me that while ministering to the People of God, the People of God will also be ministering to you without knowing it; what a beautiful exchange of gifts from God. I felt blessed in my ministry there. Thus even though I have left Lake Havasu City, I still have a piece of that place in my heart. Today I consider Lake Havasu City as a home away from home.

I would like to thank in a special way Pat and Patti Bucchino for volunteering to do the housekeeping of our rectory throughout my stay in Lake Havasu City. I thank my God for coming in contact with this wonderful family in my life pilgrimage, and I greatly enjoyed the warm friendship and company of this excellent couple. Special thanks to Jim Crawford and Toni and the many other good people of Lake Havasu City too numerous to mention in this brief work. They remind me that men are rich, not in proportion to their possessions, but to their benevolence.

At this juncture I would like to remark that moving to Phoenix was an added blessing from God to me. I have benefited from the support from the wonderful staff of the Spiritual Care Department of Banner Good Samaritan Medical Center, Phoenix, particularly, the CPE training I got under the auspices of Rev. Kelli Shepard, Rev. Adriana Cavina, and Silvia Tiznado. Other people who are in my thanking list are Quinton Britt, Maritza Vega, Rosa St. Angelo, Gail Torres, Rainey Hollayway, Juliet Gomez, and E.J. Montini, Mike Zavala, Dr. and Mrs. Paul Emeka, others are Mr. and Mrs. Matt Morgan, Virginia Onwordi, Bridget Consentino, Mr. and Mrs. Jeff Hale, Mr. and Mrs. Sebastian Onyepunuka, Mr. and Mrs. John McNulty, and others for all their support in this edition of my work. I appreciate all your encouragement. You have taught me that, by determination and kindness, you can drag an elephant with a hair.

My litany of thanks will not be complete without thanking in a special way my home Bishop from Nigeria, Most Rev. Dr. Michael Elue, whose fatherly love and affection have provided me the confidence and support to embark on this book project. I thank all my brother priests from the diocese of Issele-Uku, Nigeria, especially, Fathers John Aduba, my big brother and mentor; Rev. Sam Igwenwanne, my cousin; Msgr. S. Uzoma; Rev. Stephen Chukwuma; Msgr. Buchi Aninye; Fr. Evaristus Anene; Rev. Emmanuel Akalue; and Rev. Charles Uganwa. I want to acknowledge with gratitude the support and nurturing of my own family. To my father, Mr. Gabriel Igwenwanne, my oldest brother Isaac Igwenwanne, and my other brothers.

Listing a litany of acknowledgements for a book of this magnitude is like digging a hole for oneself. To start is easy, but to stop is difficult. Where do I stop? The gospel truth is that I just have to stop somewhere, even though I know that I will omit a host of other people too numerous to mention for want of space and time, for these I say a big thank you from the depth of my heart for their enormous contributions towards the realization of this dream. God bless you as you browse through the pages of this book.

Rev. Dr. Fidelis Igwenwanne, BCC
   Mercy Gilbert Medical Center
   3555 S. Val Vista Dr., Gilbert, AZ 85297
   480-728-8334
E-mail. Fidelisre@yahoo.com
        May 26th 2013

CONTENTS

CHAPTER I

CHAPTER II

CHAPTER III

CHAPTER IV

CHAPTER V

CHAPTER VI

CHAPTER VII
Prayer and Celebration of the Eucharist:
Key to Priestly Holiness

CHAPTER VIII
The power of the cross

CHAPTER IX
Healing the wounds of life

CHAPTER X
Mother Mary and Priests

CHAPTER XI
Lay Priesthood

CHAPTER XII
A Priest: Lover of the Poor

FOREWORD

When I was an infant, my mother thought I was going to die. You see, I became very ill after the painters for the military installation painted our living quarters. I became so ill that I was flown by helicopter to Walter Reed Medical Center. It was something to do with my lungs and the lead-based paint. The doctors took so many X-rays that they finally ordered that I could have additional X-rays only if it was absolutely necessary. To this day, they don't really know what it was; for lack of anything better, they called it "Infantile Pneumonia." It was through a glass box that my mom prayed for me and said to God, "Please let me keep him now; you can have him back later." Little did she know that God would answer this prayer and many years later call me into the wonderful and mystical service of being a priest! At my ordination, she cried as she remembered. As I began my journey into the priesthood, I heard the sage advice of my own spiritual director, that it would take me a lifetime to understand what it is to be a priest!

Father Fidelis Igwenwanne, in his new book, A Man for God and for Others, shares with you this life-long journey of coming to understand the mystical nature of who the priest is—truly a man for God and truly called to serve all! As a priest of a large parish in Mesa, Arizona, called Christ the King, I have a very large congregation to pastor. I also have the privilege to serve those affected by cancer at the Saint Peregrine Cancer Shrine at that same parish. With my years of being a priest, I could see all of Fr. Fidelis's wisdom as I reflected on my own ministry as a priest of God called to serve others. Fr. Fidelis and I met through a priest friend from Lake Havasu. Because of his sociable and fun nature, Fr. Fidelis and I became fast friends. Since then Fr. Fidelis has helped me numerous times in the parish covering Masses and Confessions. He remains a good friend and a good priest, an example to follow.

If you want to learn a bit more about the nature, history, and heart of the Catholic priesthood, I recommend you read Fr. Fidelis's book. Or you can take the "sure" road: Have your mother pray for you, and then let God work His miracle and call you into the priesthood. Just maybe you will get to know what it means to be called to serve God and others as a priest!

Rev. Stephen A. Kunkel
Pastor, Christ the King
Roman Catholic Parish, Mesa
1551 E. Dana Ave.
Mesa, Az 85204

FOREWORD

In this book, Rev. Fr. Fidelis Igwenwanne has taken a lot of pains to write with clarity A Man for God and for Others. His simple style will go a long way to help those who find holiness of life very difficult. In the book, he elucidates the fact that holiness is one of the virtues that makes us what we are and what we ought to be. Whether it is easy or difficult to live, we have to live a holy life.

The author of this book wants us to grasp the fact that holiness of life entails a lot. We have to become aware of the fact that among various possibilities open to one is holiness of life. Joy always follows for the one who lives a holy life. The author sees the call to holiness on the part of God, and the yearning for holy priests on the part of the people of God, which will be realized in the heart of the priest who applies in his own life what the ordaining Bishop commissioned on the day of his ordination. Priests are challenged in the world of today to be living examples of holiness so that "others may be drawn to our Lord Jesus Christ, the true foundation of all holiness."

It is the conviction of Fr. Fidelis that a priest cannot live in isolation because he needs others as well as a relationship with God. In the pages of this book, he spells out how this goal can be achieved. Sincerely, to read it is to draw from the wealth of experience of the author, both as a priest, as a former Director of the Emmaus School of New Evangelization, and as a chaplain.

In this book, we see that all people are yearning to learn. The priest has been chosen by Jesus to teach them. "I have called you by name: you are mine: When you pass through the water, I will be with you; in the rivers, you shall not drown. When you walk through fire, you shall not be burned; the flames shall not consume you. For I am the Lord, your God, the Holy One of Israel, your savior. You are precious in My eyes and glorious. Fear not, for I am with you" (Is. 43:1-5).

In order to derive all God's blessings through the priesthood, get this book. You will learn relevant ways of acquiring holiness of life that will bring joy, blessing, self-fulfillment and unity with God. I recommend this book to priests and seminarians, as well as lay men and women looking for a sound and up-to-the-moment spiritual book. I recommend A Man for God and for Others for you and for others.

Rev. Msgr. Dr. Stephen Uzomah
Former Rector, St. Felix Seminary
Ejeme-Aniogor. Nigeria

INTRODUCTION

Knowledge is not what happens to a person. It is what a person does with what happens to him or her. My passion for reflection on Catholic priesthood has witnessed some metamorphoses with experience, age, and time; however, the core idea on the nature of priestly life never changes. I consider this book, titled *A man for God and for Others: A Personal Reflection on the Catholic Priesthood* as the third edition of my spiritual refection on the Catholic priesthood among God's people. This book is an update of all my former works on making the nature and dignity of the Catholic priesthood known and appreciated. As a proverb says, "Experience is a comb which nature gives us when we are bald." My insight into the nature and personality of priesthood has enlarged over the years since my last edition. The present edition, in telling us that a priest is a man for God and for others, answers the question posed by the last edition titled, *A Priest: Who is He Amongst You?* The main objective here is to make available to everyone a concise idea of a priest as a man not for himself but for others. His life is that of loving service to God and to the people of God in the person of Christ, the head of the Church.

Do not expect to read this book as you might read most other books. It is designed to give you more than mere information. It offers a broader understanding and deeper appreciation of the nature of the priesthood and the personality of a priest, especially his duality as an ordinary man and as a man of God. He operates within God's people on a daily basis. The book is calculated to enlarge the readers' view of the priest's behavior so that this will strengthen their ability to love and deal more closely and realistically with priests. This book tries to help readers get the most out of experience of a priest in daily life. In fact, it is a guide to greater peace of mind and increased spiritual vitality. Its ultimate goal is a more satisfying, enlightened, and grace-filled relationship with priests throughout life that will ultimately lead you to God in the life to come. To absorb its rich message into your being will require time, reflection, application, and persevering practice.

> *The priesthood has not been transmitted by heredity. It is not something that is delegated by the people. There is only one priesthood, the priesthood of the unique son of God (Jesus Christ).*

Yes, a priest has a unique dignity and identity among Christ's faithful.

The impact of a priest upon the world impacts the whole mystical Body. In this, Christ depends upon all His members, lay people included. The understanding of what is the position of a priest among the people of God will enable them to give greater appreciation to his work. Without the power to offer sacrifice, he would not be a priest. Sacrifice and priesthood are correlative terms.

Although Christ the Priest is no longer visibly present upon earth, the fruits of His priesthood are being daily transmitted. Since our divine Lord understood perfectly the nature of man and woman and their need for visible signs and institutions, He established upon earth a visible priesthood. The priesthood has not been transmitted by heredity. It is not something that is delegated by the people. There is only one priesthood, the priesthood of the unique Son of God (Jesus Christ).

The Christian priesthood is but a participation in this, brought about by consecration or ordination. Ordination, in some respects, is for the priest what the incarnation was for Christ. In the incarnation, it was the Divinity Himself, who anointed and consecrated Christ as priest. Ordination gives the priest a share in that anointing and consecration through the character of orders and the grace of priesthood.

The relation of a priest to Christ by the sacrament of Holy Orders is a created copy of the relation that Christ has to God. Christ is the Second Person of the Most Holy Trinity. In a like manner, Christ possesses a priest by means of the character of Holy Orders and enables him to do the work of priesthood. Through the sacramental character of Holy Orders, a priest shares in the same ministry of Christ in today's world.

According to Fr. Olier, a priest is like the "Sacrament" of Jesus on earth. He has been delegated with the power to do what Christ can do. He is not only the 'Sacrament' of Jesus on earth when he is performing these powers. His priesthood is not something more or less external, an office in which he can act as functionary at required times and then put aside while he goes about living as other men in the world. His priesthood is rather an internal modification of his very being, entirely independent of his thinking and acting. He is established by His priesthood in a new and unchangeable relationship that Christ has by reason of His incarnation towards God and the Church.

A priest is at every moment of his day and night given over to God, to Jesus Christ, and to the Church in the same way as Jesus Himself served God, a state that was at the same time a state of priesthood.

The character of Holy Orders confers, as it were, a new nature, a new personality upon the priest. Priestly ordination brings about in the priest a complete identification with Jesus Christ because it makes him share in the fullness of the grace of Christ as head of the mystical Body, and because it establishes the priest with Jesus Christ as the universal mediator of religion.

Christ speaks to men through the priest's lips, blesses men through the hand of a priest, sees them through the priest's eyes, loves them through the priest's heart, helps them through the priest's hand, and teaches them through the priest's mind.

Blessed, Pope John Paul II, speaking to the priests during the Second Worldwide Retreat for Priests, said that in its essence, the priestly vocation is a call to holiness. "Holiness is an intimacy with God and an imitation of the poverty, chastity, and humility of Jesus Christ. In discharging his priestly virtues and duties, the priest should love and pasture his flock. For the priest, every single person must have importance. The care of whole communities does not dispense him from concern for the spiritual needs and specific vocations of individuals."

> *Christ speaks to men through the priest's lips, blesses men through the hand of a priest; sees them through the priest's eyes loves them through the priest's heart, helps them through the priest's hand and teaches them through the priest's mind.*

From the above statement of the pope, one can say that today, more than ever, the priest must form and educate the faithful in a personal way with spiritual direction. The priest must remember that to guide the faithful in an enlightened manner along the path of holiness, he must offer a balanced and complete teaching of the spiritual life. The priest must remember also that his vocation calls him to service and holiness.

If the priest is a saint, his people will be holy.
If he is holy, his people will be good.
If he is good, his people will be fair.
If the priest is fair, his people will be mediocre.
If the priest is mediocre, his people will be bad.

As far as I know, no priest deliberately opts for the last statement for his community. Since this is a spiritual book, it does not strictly intend to serve academic purposes as such. I have deliberately ignored some annotations and footnotes in order not to impede the flows of ideas and the spiritual meditation that follows it.

DEDICATION

In Loving memory of my mother
Cecilia Igwenwanne
and my only sister
Ngozi Rita Igwenwanne
who inspired me to dedicate my life
to the service of God as a priest.

CHAPTER I

NATURE OF THE PRIESTHOOD

Who is the lamb? The lamb of course, is the high priest and victim, Jesus Christ, who is enthroned for all eternity for the heavenly altar. In one of his visions recorded in the Book of the Revelation, St. John the Evangelist speaks in mysterious words of "the lamb who has been slain from the foundation of the world" (Rev. 13:8). From the first book of the Bible, Genesis, to the last book, Revelation, the priest and victim Christ is central: from beginning to end and in every age of time in between. From this high priest and victim flows the nature of the Catholic priesthood we have today. A priest represents Christ.

FATHERS AND DOCTORS OF THE CHURCH
ON THE NATURE OF THE PRIESTHOOD

The writing of the Fathers and Doctor's of the Church contributed decisively to shape the Christian concept of the priesthood that we have today. A few brief examples may be of help here:

- In his Epistle to the Christians of Smyrna, St. Ignatius, Martyr, says that the priesthood is the most sublime of all created dignities:
- St. Ephrem calls it an infinite dignity "The priesthood is an astounding miracle, great, immense, and infinite."
- St John Chrysostom says that though its functions are performed on earth, the priesthood should be numbered among the things of heaven.
- St. Denis calls the priest a divine man.
- St. Ambrose once said that the dignity of the priest by far exceeds that of kings, as the value of gold surpasses that of lead. His reason is that the power of kings extends only to temporal goods and to the bodies of men and women, but the power of the priests extends to spiritual goods and human souls.

The above writings of the Fathers and Doctors of the Church appreciate the mysterious nature of the Catholic priesthood today. It reminds us of the saying that states "the words of our elders are words of wisdom." Apparently, Baroness de Hueck Doherty has read the works of the Fathers of the Church when she said the following about the nature of priesthood.

- A priest encompasses all things
- The heart of a priest, like Christ's is pierced with the lance of love.
- The heart of a priest is open, like Christ's for the whole world to walk through.
- The heart of a priest is a chalice of love.
- The heart of a priest is the trusting place of human and divine love.
- A priest is a man whose goal is to be another Christ.
- A priest is a man who lives to serve.
- A priest is a man who has crucified himself, so that he too may be lifted up and draw all things to Christ.
- A priest is a man in love with God.
- A priest is the gift of God to mankind, and of mankind to God.
- A priest is a symbol of the word made flesh.
- A priest is the named sword of God's justice.
- A priest is the hand of God's mercy.
- A priest is the reflection of God's love.

No wonder St. Vincent the Paul said: "Oh, how great is a good priest, How sublime his dignity.

Vatican II on the Nature of the Priesthood

The ecclesiology of the Catholic priesthood is eloquently attested in many documents of the Second Vatican Council, especially in the Decree on the Ministry and Life of Priests (*Presbyterium Ordinis*). The document didn't mince words emphasizing the power of collaborative action of the priesthood. Here the document teaches that the function of a priest is like that of the bishops, though in a subordinate level, participates in the threefold office of Christ. In other words, as collaborators with the Order of Bishops, they share in the authority of Christ—namely the threefold authority by which Christ builds and teaches as prophet, sanctifies as priest, and governs as king. Their task is predominantly pastoral, that is to say, the care of souls. By virtue of his office, a priest is required to exercise his ministry of leadership among the community of God's people. He is the custodian of the word and sacraments. His sacramental ministry has its epitome in the Eucharist (OP 2). Emphasis is also placed on preaching in all its ramifications. The focus is in the word and sacrament, which is to assist the entire community to deepen the quality of their spiritual life and worship to God: "a living sacrifice, holy and acceptable to God" (Rom. 12:1).

Furthermore, this document reaffirms that the ordination to the priesthood is a sacrament. It states, "Through that sacrament (referring to sacrament of Holy orders), priests by the anointing of the Holy Spirit are signed with a special character and so are configured to Christ the priest in such a way that they are able to act in the person of Christ (act in *persona Christi*) the head" (OP 2). In recent years, some questions had been raised about the whole idea of the concept of *"in persona Christi."* Well, it can be argued from the testimony of the Vatican II document on priesthood and from the teaching of our most recent popes: Blessed John Paul II and Pope Benedict XVI, one will conclude that the idea of *"in persona Christi"* is still very valid in the Catholic Church. "By their sacred ordination, priests are conformed to Christ in their very being, so they can act *in persona Christi*", said Pope Benedict XII.[1] The Pope added that every priest is to recognize that his true identity is that of bringing to the world "another God Himself. God is the only treasure which ultimately people desire to find in a priest."[2] It must be noted that this concept will remain of fundamental importance in the life of the Church.

Most Recent writings on the nature of the priesthood

Recent writings and statements of the Church hierarchy are filled with endless series of quotations and statements on the nature of the priesthood.

Blessed Pope John Paul II refers to a priest as "a man of the Eucharist." (General Audience, May 12th 1993). "This man (a priest) is no way performing functions for which he is highly qualified by his natural ability nor is he doing the things that please him most and that are profitable. On the contrary,

---

1   Pope Benedict XVI, Speech in preparation for the Year for Priests, 2009.
2   Pope Benedict XVI, Year for Priests.

the one who receives that Sacrament is sent to give what he cannot give of his own strength. He is sent to act in the person of another to be his living instrument or call him a Sacrament", said Pope Benedict XVI.[3]

Cardinal Avery Dulles has one of the most intriguing statements of our time. In his article titled "Priest and Eucharist: No Higher Calling," he writes:

> I like to think that priesthood is more a matter of being than doing. At ordination the priest receives an indelible mark that makes him different—"ontologically" different, some prefer to say—no matter whether he does anything or not. Even if he performed no priestly ministry, he would still be a priest forever. He is ordained in order to perform a specific service toward the Lord and towards the people of God.[4]

During his homily at the 2010 priestly ordination at the Cathedral of SS. Simon and Jude, in Phoenix, Bishop Thomas Olmsted, the Bishop of Phoenix and the ordaining prelate addressed the *ordinandi* in the following words:

> From this day forward, the faithful of the Church will call you "Father." They will do this because God Himself is giving you the grace today to share in His Fatherhood, and to love others in His name. As a true spiritual father, then, listen with compassion to all whom you serve; welcome the stranger as a son or daughter in Christ; lift up and defend the rights of the unborn child, the elderly who are forgotten, and the immigrant whose human dignity is overlooked.[6]

Msgr. Stephen J. Rossetti has written and published a lot of works on priesthood, He once said in one of his books that "the priest himself is sacramentally immolated to the measure that Christ dwells in him."[5]

Priestly ordination conveys in the priest a complete identification with Jesus Christ, because it renders him a participant in the fullness of the grace of Christ as head of the mystical body, and because it establishes the priest with Jesus Christ.

---

3   This was a speech given by Pope Benedict XVI, then Cardinal Joseph Ratzinger, Prefect of the Congregation for the Doctrine of the Faith, Vatican 1990. p. 4
4   SJ Rossetti, *Born of the Eucharist: A Spirituality for Priests*, Ave Maria Press, Notre Dame 2009, p. 11.
5   SJ Rossetti, *Born of the Eucharist: A Spirituality for Priests*, p. 86.
6   Homily of Bishop Thomas Olmsted , Bishop of Phoenix addressing the Ordinandi during the 2010 priestly ordination in Phoenix, Arizona

Priesthood as a vocation of service: A man for God and for others

The Book of Hebrews provides us with the biblical foundation of the nature of priesthood as a servant who is chosen from among men to serve others as a representative of God. As the Book of Hebrews puts it, "Every high priest is taken from among men and made their representative before God, to offer gifts and sacrifice for sin" . . . and one does not take the honor upon himself, but is called by God just as Aaron was."[7]

From the above, one can say with all certainty that a Catholic priest is a man who has been called and chosen by God to serve the Church in the person of Christ the head. From the grace bestowed on him in ordination, he is intimately united to Christ. He is the lover of God, the Church, and the people he serves. This assertion bears credence from the teaching of Pope Benedict XVI. In the Pope's own words:

> In order to transmit the presence of God to others, the priest must himself be interiorly transformed and conformed to Christ, the God-man, not only by the sacramental grace of his ordination, but also by his intimate union with Christ. His mission must in turn derive essentially from that divine intimacy, in which the priest is called to be an expert, so that he may be able to lead the souls entrusted to him humbly and trustfully to the same encounter with the Lord.[8]

Every priest is a priest not for himself but for others. He is God's true presence in the world. His priesthood is an authoritative and unique way of life, which provides for the spiritual needs of others. All the priest's activities flow from the *pasch*, Christ, and also mirrors Christ through the exercise of his love in devotion, prayer and adoration, preaching the word, offering the Eucharistic sacrifice, and administrating the other sacrament. Thus through this, he increases God's glory and man's growth in the divine life.[9]

---

7   Heb. 5:1-2, 4.
8   This was an address from Pope Benedict XVI to the Congregation for Clergy in preparation for the Year for Priests, June 19, 2009 - June 19, 2010. This year also coincides with the 150th Anniversary of St. Jean Marie Vianney, patron of parish priests. The Holy Father intended to extend this patronage now to all priests, making the Holy Cure the Patron of all priests,
9   Cf. P.O. 2

Highlights of the dignity of the priestly powers

The dignity of the priest is valued from the power that he has over the real and the mystical body of Jesus Christ.

—   With regard to the power of priests over the body of Jesus Christ, it is of faith that when they pronounce the words of consecration the incarnate Word has obliged himself to obey and to come into their hands under the sacramental species.

—   We were struck with wonder when we hear that God obeyed the voice of Joshua, "Stand still, O sun, at Gibeon, O moon, in the valley of Aijalon! And the sun stood still, and the moon stayed while the nation took vengeance on its foes."[10]

But our wonder should be far greater when we find that in obedience to the words of His priests—*Hoc Est Corpus Meum* (This is my body—God Himself descends on the altar. He comes whenever they call Him, and as often as they call Him. He places Himself in their hands, even though they could be in sin. And after having come, He remains entirely at their disposal: they move him as they please, from one place to another; they may, if they wish, shut Him up in the tabernacle, or expose Him on the altar, or carry Him outside the Church; they may if they choose, eat His flesh and give Him as food for others. "Oh how very great is their power," says St. Laurence, speaking of priests. A word falls from their lips, and the body of Christ—substantially formed from the matter of bread and the incarnate word descended from heaven—is found really present on the table of the altar. Never did Divine goodness give such power to the angels. The angels abide by the order of God, but the priests take Him in their hands, distribute Him to the faithful, and partake of Him as food for themselves.

Why are priests called vicars of Christ? This is because they hold His place on earth. "You hold the place of Christ," says St. Augustine. "You are His lieutenants."

In the council of Milan, St. Charles Borromeo called priests the representatives of the person of God on earth. Before him the apostles speak "for Christ; we are ambassadors."[11]

When he ascended into heaven, Jesus Christ left His priests after Him to hold on earth His place of mediator between God and men, particularly on the

---

10   Jos. 10:12
11   Cor. 5 : 20

altar. "Let the priests," says St. Laurence Justinian, "approach the altar as another Christ." St. Cyprian concurs: "A priest at the altar performs the office of Christ."

The priest holds the place of the savior Himself when, by saying *"Ego tu absoluo,"* (I absolve you) he absolves sinners from sin. This great power, which Jesus Christ has received from his eternal father, He has communicated to His priests.[12]

According to Tertullian, Jesus invests the priests with His own powers. To pardon a single sin requires all the omnipotence of God. The Jews were aware of this, hence, when they heard that Jesus Christ pardoned the sins of the paralytic, the Jews justly said "who can forgive sins but God alone?" But what only God can do by His omnipotence, the priest can also do by saying *"Ego tu absoluo a peccatis tuis."* In the form of the sacraments, the words produce what they signify.

The priest, by saying *"Ego te absoluo,"* changes the sinner from an enemy into the friend of God and from the slave of hell into an heir of paradise. In this same way, by saying "This is my body," the priest changes the bread and wine into the body and blood of Jesus. It is important to note that the more the faithful take advantage of the sacrament of reconciliation, the holier the priests become.

That is why priests should be afraid of falling. It is a scandal for the person of such sublime dignity to wallow in sin. Lamenting, St. Gregory cries out: "Pacified by the hands of the priest the elect enters the heavenly country, and alas; priests precipitate themselves into the fire of hell."

The priest's call to holiness

A call to holiness brings to mind a beautiful scriptural passage addressed to the whole people of God, but having special meaning for God's priests: "You should be holy to me; for I the Lord am holy and have separated you from the people, that you should be mine.[13]

Though all the faithful are called to holiness, there is a special need and urgency on the part of the priest to be holy. Canon law thus expresses it in these words: "Clerics are bound to lead a more saintly interior life than the laity, and to give them example by excelling in virtue of righteous conduct."

---

12   Tom Forrest; *A Call to Holiness*, Redemption Press London, 1984 p 82.
13   Lev. 20 : 26; Mtt. 5 : 48

According to late Bishop Godfrey Mary Paul Okoye CSSP, "a priest has two wings with which to fly to heaven, the wing of holiness and the wing of knowledge. He must be holy, for God is holy. He must be a man of knowledge, for he is a leader of the people. He must strive all his life to maintain these two wings intact."[14]

1. THE PRIEST IS APPOINTED FOR MEN IN THE THINGS THAT PERTAIN TO GOD (HEB 5:1).

St. Thomas Aquinas says that those who are mediators between God and mankind must have a good conscience before God and a good name before men and women. It is sad and unfortunate that many priests have lost their credibility before God and mankind.

If the priest does not make himself everyday more pleasing to God, how dare he enter the court of the Lord? For what companionship has light with darkness? On the other hand, if before mankind the priest appears as a trustee of the holy things he handles and preaches, how does he expect people to believe and value what his conduct and way of life repudiate? That is why the psalmist prayed, "Let thy priests, O Lord, be clothed with justice and let thy servants rejoice."[15]

In praying for priests during the Last Supper, Jesus spoke of them as gifts given by the Father for continuing His mission. And He makes it clear that they can succeed in doing this only by retaining a oneness with Him. "I am the vine, you are the branches. He who lives in me and I in him, will produce abundantly. . . . I pray for those you have given me . . . that they may be one even as we are one. . . . guard them from the evil one . . . as you sent them into the world, so I may be consecrated in truth."[16]

The same thought is echoed by the anointing of the Holy Spirit. Priests are marked with a special character and are so configured to Christ the priest that they can act in the person of Christ the head . . . to build up and establish his whole body which is the Church.[17]

---

14   Bishop G.M.P.: Okoye, Priestly Life. p. 52
15   Ps. 132:9
16   Jn. 15:5; 17 - 19
17   Vatican II, *Presbyterium Ordinis* 2:12

2. THE PRIEST IS VISIBLE SIGN AND LIVING INSTRUMENT OF CHRIST.

A priest is required to be a sign that he signifies. The priest in his life and work is for the people the visible embodiment of Christ the High Priest.

Priests should be holy, because God has placed them in the word as models of virtue.

- They are called by St. John Chrysostom, "Teachers of Piety."
- St. Peter Chrysologus calls them the "model of virtue."
- St. Isidore says, "Whoever leads people on the road of virtue must himself be holy and blameless."
- St. Gregory says that the hand that must wash away the stains and defilement of others must not be polluted. In another place, he says that the torch that does not burn, cannot inflame others.
- Archbishop Fulton J. Sheen in his book titled "A Priest is not his own" explicates that like Christ a priest is a "Holy victim" through offering himself as a victim, the priest continually makes His incarnation persistently present to the world.

Sr. Bridget McKenna, a sister of the Poor Clares, who dedicates her life to ministering to priests all over the world, once said that nobody on earth has the powers and spiritual gifts that the priest has. Highlighting some of the these powers, she added: To them belongs the power to forgive sin, that is the gift of reconciliation with God and fellow men; the power to preach, heal and satisfy hunger, by feeding the people of God; the gift of the Eucharist, where the priest exercises his power of changing bread and wine into the body of Jesus; the power of intercession.

In addition she said that the hand of a priest is anointed and that every time a priest blesses, he heals and intercedes. She cites an incident of a girl whose protracted head disease disappeared after a blessing from a priest.

3. THE PRIEST IS THE DISCIPLE AND APOSTLE OF CHRIST

The priest is a man who has first received a call from Christ, who has learned at the feet of the Lord, and now has been sent out to men to represent the Lord and to teach them to observe "whatever I have commanded you."[18]

The priest conveys to others his own living and vibrant faith, his own enthusiastic love and knowledge of God and his Christ. His qualification comes from what John says in his first letter:

> That which was from the beginning, which we have heard, which we have seen with our eyes, which we have looked upon and touched with our hands, concerning the word of life—the life was made manifest, and we saw it, and testify to it, and proclaim to you the eternal life which was with the Father and was made manifest to us–that which we have seen and heard we proclaim also to you, so that you may have fellowship with us; and our fellowship is with the Father and with his Son Christ.[19]

That is, the priest must be a living witness to that Christ whom he preaches, and he preaches as one who has first welcomed in himself the realities which he preaches.

4. THE PRIEST IS THE STEWARD OF GOD'S MYSTERIES, ESPECIALLY OF EUCHARIST

They who are not holy should not handle holy things (St. Thomas Aquinas). The mysteries of God are concerned with the increase of holiness and union with God among the people and their effectual salvation. These gifts of God come to the people through the priest, as he is admonished on the day of ordination.

Priests cannot disperse the sacred mysteries as if they were tunnels through which grace passes without leaving any mark. They must first open themselves to the spiritual realty to which they minister. Thus the injunction, imitate what you handle.

Lumen Gentium

Lumen Gentium demands one and the same holiness of every member of the Church. And this common holiness is characterized by four qualities:

---

18   Mt. 28:19
19   I Jn. 1:1-3

our submission to the guidance of the Holy Spirit; our obedience to the voice of the Father; our worship of the Father in spirit and truth, and our faithfulness in following the poor, humble, and cross-bearing Christ.[20]

But since the priests must be the first to carry out their ministry with holiness, the Vatican II Council's Decree on the Ministry and Life of Priests lists eight added means at the disposal of priests for fostering personal holiness:

- Constant nourishment at the twin tables of God's word and the Holy Eucharist.
- Fruitful and frequent reception of the sacrament of reconciliation.
- Spiritual reading done with a faith that leads to discerning God's will, and docility following the impulses of grace.
- Devotion to Mary as the perfect model of docility.
- Daily visits to the blessed sacraments.
- Regular spiritual retreats.
- Faithfulness to spiritual direction.
- A habit of prayer centered on the cry of adoration "Abba Father."[21]

---

20   Vatican II Dogmatic Constitution on the Church *Lumen Gentium* 1964, No. 14 p. 365.
21   Vat. II, Decree on the Ministry and Life of Priests *Presbyterium Ordinis* 1965, No. 18. p. 897,

CHAPTER II

YOU AND YOUR PRIEST

The way a priest goes to a parish is through the Bishop's assignment. He arrives and reports to duty in his capacity as the pastor, parochial vicar, or priest in residence. You the parishioners call him "father," because he is your spiritual father. You see him almost every day if you are a morning Mass goer or weekly if you go to Mass every Sunday, serving you as the servant of Christ and your own servant and father. His role is that of "spiritual fatherhood" more than anything else. He plays these roles when he says Mass for you, exhorts you in his homilies, offers you the Body and Blood of Jesus, reconciles you to God in the Sacrament of Reconciliation, blesses you with his hands, advises you in spiritual direction and counseling, and leads you to God through the administration of other sacraments. He is God's representative among you. Parishioners develop an unforgettable experience of their priests in the parish, especially the impact he makes on them daily. Having said this, it is up to every parishioner to answer the following questions: Can you easily relate with your priests? In other words, who is your priest for you as a person? Do you have a hard time when it comes to understanding or relating to your priests? Maybe all you need to do is to strive to know your priests a little bit. The following pages may offer you some of the tools you need. It might lead you to have some glimpse of the personality of the priests in your daily life in the parish.

KNOW YOUR PRIESTS

As with the Sacred Host, the priest is the sign of a divine reality, and, at the same time, hides it. To recognize God in the person of His ministers, reason is inadequate; one must believe. One must acknowledge that beneath the surface there is something ineffable that infinitely transcends what can be seen and imagined. The spirit of faith which you will need "in order to look upon your priests as ministers of Christ" (I Cor. 4:1) requires first of all that you understand them "They are men like you, but taken from among men for things of God."[22]

The priest is subject to the limitations of weakness like the rest of men; this is precisely why he makes sin offering (sacrifices) first of all for himself and for other people (Heb. 5:3). He is appointed to act on your behalf in relationship with God, to offer gifts and sacrifices for sin (Heb. 5:1, 8:3).

A big step will be made in the right directions when Christians laymen and women who ordinarily know little about the priest—his material difficulties, his isolation, his psychology— will put him on the real plane of his mysterious duality, where he is both one of them and the transcendent envoy of the Lord. One of the first duties of Catholics is to grasp again the meaning of the priesthood. It is up to them, and only at the price of this understanding, to reinstate the priest in his proper place in society.

PRAY FOR YOUR PRIESTS

In our last Chrism Mass (Maundy Thursday, the anniversary of the Catholic Priesthood), Bishop Olmsted, reading from the Rite of Renewal of Commitment to Priestly Service, enjoined all the people of God present to pray for their priests in the following words: "My brothers and sisters, pray for your priests. Ask the Lord to bless them with fullness of love, to help them to be faithful ministers of Christ the High Priest, so that they will be able to lead you to him, the fountain of salvation."[23] Here, the Church tells us that priests need a lot of prayers and invites us through the voice of our bishop, the shepherd and the successor of the Apostles for the Diocese of Phoenix, to pray earnestly for priests. One may be tempted to ask, why pray especially for priests, while all people need prayers? Well, there are many reasons why we should pray for priests in a special way even though all need prayers. Praying for priests hinges on the "fullness of love" for the ministry so they can be dedicated ministers in the Lord's vineyard. The need for prayers for priests cannot be over-emphasized. Priests need prayers because of the spiritual role they play among God's people. Prayer is the key to holiness and success in all the spiritual endeavors of a priest. The spiritual load of a priest in the parish can be very challenging; hence spiritual support

---

22   Heb. 5:2
23   Bishop Thomas Olmsted, Bishop of Phoenix at the Renewal of Commitment to Priestly service at Chrism Mass at SS Simon and Jude Cathedral, April 2nd 2012.

through prayer is imperative.

As spiritual leaders, priests lead people of God to God; in view of this, they need to remain faithful to the end. Their spiritual role can be complex to understand. As Cardinal Avery Dulles puts it, "Priesthood is more a matter of being than doing. At ordination, the priest receives an indelible mark that makes him different–'ontologically' different." This remark asserts the duality in the priestly personality. He is a man of God and an ordinary man at the same time. Due to this duality, people get confused about the complexity of the priest's presence. Some make the common mistake of dehumanizing the priesthood and, consequently, of setting the priest outside of ordinary life. While others, over-humanize him and consequently rob him from the Divine life. The truth is that the priest "walks before the face of the All Holy."[24] He is a mystery. And yet he is a man that is susceptible to fall from human frailty and human fragility. A lot of prayers are needed that God will shelter him in his wings. According to Baroness de Hueck Doherty, "The heart of a priest, like Christ's, is pierced with the lance of love. He is a lover of God and lover of men [and women]."[25] It is never too late to start praying for your priests. You can spiritually adopt a priest by praying with his name or praying for priests in general. Believe it or not, priests are grateful for all the prayer networks going on already here in the Diocese of Phoenix, both collectively and individually. Coming to mind right away is the Serra Club and Knights of Columbus, who pray and support priests and the vocation to the priesthood. Furthermore, certain individuals and families at the parish level have committed to praying for priests, for seminarians, and for vocations here in the Diocese of Phoenix. For example, at Christ the King Parish in Mesa, AZ, there exists an organized program of praying for vocations, where families are assigned officially with a symbolic gesture (a chalice) with which to pray a week's prayer time. The family comes forward and receives a special blessing from a priest at Sunday Mass. Please join the bandwagon to pray for priests and vocations, and God will bless you abundantly.

---

24   Baroness de Hueck Doherty, Good Priest. http://prayersforpriests.homestead.com/
25   Baroness de Hueck Doherty, Good Priest.

TRYING TO ARISE ABOVE HUMAN WEAKNESS

St. John Chrysostom once said: he who honors a priest honors Christ, he who insults a priest insults Christ.

It appears that some think that angels alone should be appointed to this high office and yet God has sent for the ministry of resuscitation, not angels, but men: He has not sent . . . beings of some unknown nature and some strange blood, but of your own bone and your own flesh. . . . He has appointed sons of Adam, men like unto us, exposed to the same temptations.

That is why the letter of Hebrews tells us that a priest is able to have compassion on the ignorant and erring, because he himself also is beset with weakness, and by reason therefore is obliged to "make sin offerings for himself as well as for the people".[26] Mother Teresa once said:

> When a priest, groaning in spirit at his own unworthiness and at the loftiness of his office, places his consecrated hands upon our hands; when, humiliated at finding himself the dispenser of the Blood of the covenant; each time amazed as he pronounces the words that give life, when a sinner has absolved a sinner; we, who rise from our knees before him, feel we have done nothing abasing… We have been at the face of a man who represented Jesus Christ… We have been there to receive the dignity of free men and sons of God.[27]

You must not forget that priests are, and that they remain, men. God does not perform a miracle to wrest them from the human state. The priesthood does not of itself give a person the power to do everything or to excel in everything. It is important to remember this, lest you fall into a very old error, that of dehumanizing the priesthood and consequently of setting the priest outside of ordinary life. That does great harm to him, by thus isolating him as unbelievers do, to the exclusive realm of ceremonies. He is deprived in good part of his reason for being. If men refuse to pass through him, he no longer can be, at least fully, their mediator.

Whatever his admittedly human faults may be, of this you can be sure: he does love his people, and he does worry about them, including you. Because

---

26   Heb. 5:23
27   Tom Forrest, *Call to Holiness*, p. 59

he can never forget that one day he is going to give an account to his Master for every one of you. He may hide his feelings well, but there will be many a night when he will lie on his bed and look at the ceiling, reflecting that he is not a better priest and ashamed that so many of his parishioners are leading more Christ-like lives.

He will think of his faults, and as he counts them over, he will think of the magnitude of his calling, the love of service in his heart,   the reverence, the consideration and respect that people show him in the   parish, in offices, by government officials, etc, in spite of everything. He feels overwhelmed and gives glory to God for calling him to be a priest despite his weakness as a man. Then he arises and strives to be good. It can be reflected that one of the reasons we priests are trying to be good is precisely because of the high ideals Catholics have of the priesthood, and one of the reasons why we do keep trying to arise above our human weakness is because our people–as well as God–expect it of us. As the moonbeam moves across the room, and his eyes grow heavy, he will be both grateful and humble. Grateful to you and all his people, who give so much and expect so little. Humble in his own eyes, that he has done so little with so much, and he will fall asleep with a prayer on his lips: "Lord God, be good to them; make up for my failings. Don't let them suffer through my neglects; and please, dear Jesus, help me to be more like what I ought to be." I know that it happens to others because it happens to me.

Some are caught up with saying unkind things about their priests that may seem insignificant in themselves. And frequently, too, these remarks do more harm than the one who makes them realizes or imagines. It is an attack on the priesthood in general. Such Catholics might learn from our Protestant friends. Let such Catholics try once to speak unkindly to a Protestant about his or her minister, and most Protestants will resent such an affront. They don't accept it because they deem it an insult against their whole religious faith, which it is in fact. How grave the offence of a priest who enjoys gossips and criticisms against a fellow priest from lay members of Christ's faithful.

But what about bad priests who have dishonored the priesthood? To my mind, there is nothing more pitiful than a priest who has fallen from grace. "The higher the rise, the harder the fall," is certainly most true of an unfortunate priest. And the greatest curse upon any parish is the so-called "bad priest." Should that ever happen, rather than censure the priest, look upon it as a visitation from God upon that parish. The faithful should remember that the priest acts Ex opera operantis (out of the work of the worker). Let the great Emperor Constantine be our guide. He had so great veneration for a priest that he said: "If I should see a priest committing a fault, so far should I be from making it known that I would rather cover him with my imperial mantle, in order that men might not take scandal to the detriment of religion."[28]

> *"The unworthiness of a few cannot dim the splendor of the office." And while there is one unfortunate priest, we find thousands of good ones.*

It is true that there is no state without its stain. Angels in heaven sinned; so did Adam and Eve in the state of innocence. What of Kings Solomon and David? Judas sold Jesus for the price of a slave, and Peter denied him. Hence, while we must never excuse the sin; we must excuse the sinner. In every mistake, let us not only remember the man, but also the dignity of the man. The latter can never be taken from even an unfortunate priest.

In the words of Pope Pius XI, "The unworthiness of a few cannot dim the splendor of the office." And while there is one unfortunate priest, we find thousands of good ones. Because a few unfortunate couples have violated their vows, is not enough reason to conclude that every married man and woman violate them. Because there is one dishonest business man, we must not argue that all business men are dishonest; because one doctor is a malpractitioner, it would be wrong to declare that all physicians are scoundrels. Let us be equally fair in our reasoning with our priests. As long as we are human mortals, priests are not immune from temptations, and the priest is no exception. And perhaps because a priest knows how to sympathize with others who are tempted, that may be the reason God did not choose angels but men for the office of the priesthood.

---

28   Ryan Williams, *The other Christ*, p. 95

RESPECT YOUR PRIESTS

The priest is another Christ; respect him. He is God's representative; trust him. He is your benefactor; be thankful to him. At the altar he offers your prayers to God; do not forget him. He is the doctor of your souls; visit him.

He prays for you, and yours in purgatory; ask God's mercy from him. In the confessional, he is the physician of your soul; show him your wounds. He is a judge, although not judgmental; abide by his decision. In his daily life, he is human; do not condemn him. He is human; words of kindness will cheer him.

If you must tell his faults, tell them to God that He may give him light and strength to correct them.

While spiritual fatherhood imposes upon the priest, there are also responsibilities and faithful duties of children. They are bound to love, honor, and respect the fathers of their spiritual lives. When the faithful begin to see the priest as he really is, the father and guardian of their souls, they will rush to him with all their problems, and much of the evil and unhappiness which results from a lack of paternal care and advice will be avoided. Those who are wracking their brains for a curse for the evils of our times and especially for the delinquency of the young should look well to this close relationship between priest and people. In the spiritual life, if all men, women and children find in their priests as all-loving fathers who are eagerly awaiting to help them, evils will be eradicated and progress in virtue and happiness will come and come quickly.

The spirit of faith ought to prompt a deep respect for the man of God. Such respect is not, by any means, a servile respect as though the clergy were a special cast. Instead, it is a religious respect that can be given with wholesome simplicity. The faithful should not, however, content themselves with just feeling respect. There must be an act of deference, a homage rendered to the majesty of God's presence in His ministers. It is a gesture as well of gratitude toward our Lord for His kindness in perpetuating Himself in the world in the form that is most accessible to us, that of a man like ourselves. These dispositions of faith must not remain purely inferior but should expose themselves in a practical manner. Mothers of families will know how to instill in their children, right from their earliest childhood, habits of special courtesy towards the ministers of God. This is one of the most charming features of Catholic countries. Catholic parents should see to it that the priesthood is honored in their homes. You should welcome the priests there as you would our Lord Himself. Make them home cooked meals at your homes, or take them out to dinner and draw from their awesome Divine presence many blessing of the Lord who said, "Whoever receives you receives me, and whoever receives me receives the one who sent me. Whoever receives a prophet because he is a prophet will receive a prophet's reward. . . . And whoever gives only a cup of cold water to one of these little ones to drink because he is a disciple, Amen, I say to you, he will surely not lose his reward" (Mt.10:40-42). Catholics who welcome priests on a regular basis to their homes can testify to the inner spiritual nourishment they derive from every visit, from the beginning to the end of this visit. Catholics should bear in mind that, quite logically, they owe to the ambassador or the highest sovereign the honors that governments of this world extend to the representatives of earthly powers. They should from their hearts pay the priest their highest tribute of respect. St. Francis of Assisi said: "If I see an angel and a priest, I would bend my knee first to the priest and then the angel."[29]

LOVE AND TAKE CARE OF YOUR PRIESTS

St. Theresa, the Little Flower, once exclaimed, "Oh! How I love the priesthood."[30]

How do you behold a priest standing at the altar in sacrificial robe, celebrating? A priest is a chalice of love and reflection of God's love, so don't be disturbed or think otherwise if you see those who love him and admire his dignity flocking to him (men, women, boys and girls, children). They want to feel and enjoy the sense of holiness radiating from the presence of a priest. No matter how close the ties of affection may be, the priest moves through his people, amongst them but not of them.

Take care of your priests, said Cardinal Emmanuel Suhard, not so as to reverse the roles, for the priest is responsible for you, but to help him with

29   Ryan Williams, *The other Christ*, p. 105
30   Life of St. Thomas

his mission of authority and life. Your priests are poor; you must help them live. They have forsaken everything for you, frequently giving up a career comparable or superior to your own. You must do everything in your power to relieve the priests of their administrative tasks and even of the menial chores that take up their time and strength, much to the detriment of their interior life and ministry.

You must facilitate their endeavors. You must offer them your arms, your time, your houses, your culture. You must discreetly watch over their health. Finally, you are to be generous in giving material assistance. This is partly an act of charity, but mostly a matter of strict justice. It is not up to your priests to demand it; you must take the initiative in supporting the Church. But you must not confine your co-operation to material assistance; you must create an atmosphere of spiritual affection, reserved yet sincere.

CO-OPERATE WITH YOUR PRIEST

In all the papal encyclicals of modern times, the Holy Fathers have made it clear that the lay apostolate is not a voluntary thing which one may or may not join, like a club. On the contrary, this apostolate is today's offensive for Christ and, unless we sheepishly choose to play the role of rear-guard Christians who huddle in the bomb shelters while the battle of the souls are lost, we must hurry to the offensive. In an hour of crisis the Church calls for generous service. It is not ours to stand apart and utter eloquent condemnation of the social evils of a world that must anyhow go on. Rather, it is the task of the Christian to plunge into the disorder and to work selflessly in the endless task of setting a better example, of counseling and encouraging, of seeking and finding God in every man. Yet the offensive lags. Relatively few have carried it on to reach the vigor needed to conquer for Christ. The employers and the students must come, the generous apostles who will bring the guidance of Christ's moral teachings into the labor movement, into management, into business, into social work, into the professions, and into all other fields of human endeavors.

Catholic teaching and example must be carried into families, into offices, into factories, into civil and social life. For this work, the bishop needs not only his priests, but also his lay helpers. He knows, however, that these lay apostles too must be trained for this great responsibility. They must be men and women of great sense and rugged piety. They must be prudent and well versed in the truths of our faith.

It is of capital importance to pray for priests and with priests. After you (laity) have relieved your ministers by taking charge of the work which belongs to the laity in the plan of pastoral and temporal things that will not be the end. The Church expects you to work along with priests in a common apostolate. In doing so, you must avoid excesses in two directions: that of letting your priests do everything themselves, through scrupulousness or timidity on your part, and that of trying to supplement them, even though your intentions are good.

Through the whole mystical Body, Christ depends upon all His members (priests and lay people). Nowhere is this concept clearer than in the documents of the second Vatican Council and the writings of the popes.

Political Life

Negatively, political life is plagued by irresponsibility of many sorts. Affirmatively, democratic government is political life at its best. Pius XII tells us that politics is the work of a mature Christian. Deep involvement in politics as it is today is the field of lay faithful. Our Christians are encouraged to participate actively in politics and exemplify themselves as light of the world and salt of the earth.

The priest casts his vote, but he is not in politics, holds no political appointment, and is elected to no political office.

Family Life

Family life is of unequivocal importance for both the Church and civil society. The Second Vatican Council calls it "the vital cell of the society.[31]

It is a known fact that family life is threatened, more than threatened, from many sides in our world today. In the light of the above fact, Christian parents are called to be "cooperators of grace and witnesses of the faith"[32] to their children. This means that they are invited not only to pass on the faith to their children but also to educate them in it.

---

31   VATICAN II, Decree on the Apostolate of laity, Apostolicam Actuositatem, November 18, 1965: AAS 58, 11
     (1966), pp. 837-864.
32   AA 11

The above mentioned field goes to laymen and women by no default. They are rather the provinces of ordinary human life from which the priest is wisely subtracted so that the dedication to his altogether necessary work of souls might be more complete. Yet, the priest has interest and spiritual responsibility for the families entrusted to his care. The priest here is a cooperator of grace in nourishing the spiritual wellbeing of family life. The parish is like a school and a home at the same time. The family life is also a school. No wonder the Church teaches that parents are the "first teachers" of their children. A school is a place of learning. So also in the family and in the parish we learn values, and faith, things about God and our lives in Christ called spiritual life. At home we live and eat, so also in the parish during Mass two outstanding things happen to us: we are nourished by the Word of God and by the Sacrament of the body and blood of Christ. Then we go back to the community to live out our life of faith by bearing the authentic witness of Christian life.

In their lives, Christians are all called to advance further by deepening their faith by taking extra classes in recognized institutes approved by the Church so that they can implant this faith to others as catechists, evangelizers, youth leaders, and coordinators of various parish programs. The Church needs lay apostles: men and women trained with Christian minds—men and women with keen and unremitting apostolic skills and sense that will translate the judgment of those minds to practical action.

In this new era of evangelization, the distressing problem remains: "How shall they believe him of whom they have not heard? And how shall they hear without someone to preach? And how can they preach unless they are sent?"[33]

From this, there naturally follows the necessity of training our lay faithful to equip them to collaborate with their priests. In the Diocese of Phoenix, Kino Institute has been of invaluable service in the training of lay faithful for parish ministries. Again the establishment and running of schools of evangelization in some dioceses has yielded a lot of fruits in this direction. By way of definition, schools of evangelization[34] are programs that seek to provide a systematic training on the skills of evangelization, over an extended period of time.[35]

---

33   Rom. 10:14
34   Schools of Evangelization was inspired by the clarion call of Blessed Pope John Paul II, who is the coined the word New Evangelization and declared the Era of New Evangelization: According to Pope John Paul II, New Evangelization has to do with exploring new ways of Evangelization that must be new in zeal, new in methon and new in expression.
35   +A.O. Gbuji, New Evangelization in Nigeria Ten Years after Pope's visit, 1992.

These schools will help you (priests) obtain collaborators capable of multiplying your strength and capacity in the parish ministry. Hence the great importance is the apostolate of the laity which, as you yourselves know from your own experience, can become a powerful source of good. These schools are of paramount importance to train the lay faithful in the know-how of evangelization to equip them with useful skills. As we see in ordinary life, one cannot be a practicing doctor unless he or she qualifies from the school of medicine. One cannot be a practicing lawyer unless he or she qualifies from the law school, or a nurse unless he or she qualifies from the school of nursing. In the same way, one cannot be an evangelizer in the real sense of the word without qualifying from a school of evangelization. It must be noted that this argument does not in any way diminish the call to evangelize that all Christians received by virtue of Baptism, but enhances it.

Today, we have reason to thank God Almighty for the increasing number of lay apostolates: laity who more than ever before are being aware of their roles as God's people. Yes, the laity have a call to sanctity and to the apostolate. It is encouraging to discover that at present many generous Christians are enrolled in Catholic organizations, associations, and pious societies. In addition there are many others, although not members of organizations, who are equally ready to assist the priest in his care of souls. Therefore, it is necessary to find these individuals in order to tap their talents and skills after they have been solidly trained. The Church is always in need and continues to ever invite more generous Christians to step forward as the work of God is plentiful but the laborers are not enough. This means that the work of evangelization is inexhaustible.

No wonder St. Vincent the Paul said:"Oh, how great is a good priest. How sublime his dignity."

Priests and Deacons in the Catholic Church

It must be noted right away that deacons and priests are ordained members of Holy Orders. As such, they are both participants of the clerical state in the Church. One cannot fully grasp the correlativeness and the divergences of the above realities without first of all exploring the meaning of the Church

---

36   Cf. OP 2

hierarchy. There are three tiers or three levels of the Church hierarchy. The fullest level is the order of bishops, followed by the order of priests and then the order of deacons.

To a bishop belongs the fullness of Holy Orders.[36] By his consecration, he belongs to the college of bishops as the successor of the Apostles, so one can say that bishops are the apostles of today.

Each diocese is led by a bishop in an ecclesiastical jurisdiction, called the diocese, with many parishes under it. A bishop's main church is called the cathedral, because that is where his seat is. Here, one may like to ask, what of the pope? What of the cardinals and the archbishops. Well the answer is that the pope is also a bishop, unlike the other bishops; his ecclesiastical leadership covers the entire world. Furthermore, the pope is the Bishop of Rome. It might be surprising for some to learn that the pope's cathedral is not St. Peter's Basilica, Rome, but St. John Lateran, also in Rome. In the same token, cardinals and archbishops are also bishops of their own dioceses, or they hold special offices in the Church.

The second level of hierarchy belongs to the priesthood. A priest has less authority than a bishop. As coworker and collaborator to the order of Bishops, a priest shares in the authority of Christ. Like the bishop, a priest participates in the sacerdotal dignity. Thus he is known as "the minister of the sacrament and the Eucharist."[37] A priest is called to retain a collaborative action with his bishop. Together they form a united presbyterate (unum presbyterium). A priest leads the parish and can perform almost all the sacraments or rituals that a bishop can perform,(either by virtue of priestly ordination or by delegation, except for three rites: the sacrament of the Holy Orders (ordination to the priesthood or diaconate); consecration of the Oil of Chrism; and anointing of the church or altar with Chrism.

The deaconate, the last level, is also a very important tier of the hierarchy. A deacon has less authority than a priest and a bishop. The order of deaconate can be transitional (a transitional deacon will become a priest) or permanent(he will not become priest). In both cases, ordination convenes on them powers to function in the ministry of the word, divine worship, pastoral governance, and the service of charity. This they carry under the authority of their bishop.(Service is what defines the deaconate ministry.)

---

37   OP 5

It must be noted that deacons assist the bishops and the priests in celebrating the Holy Eucharist. While assisting at Mass, the deacon has a specific tasks: proclamation of the Gospel, preaching at times, distribution of Holy Communion, and announcing some lines reserved for him whenever he assists at Mass. Furthermore, deacons can preside over some sacraments that priests perform, namely: Baptism, blessing Marriages, and Funerals. The Sacrament of Anointing of the Sick, Celebration of the Holy Eucharist and Sacrament of Reconciliation are reserved for priests and bishops.

PRIESTS AND KNIGHTS OF COLUMBUS

A young priest was telling his story about the Knights of Columbus in the parish of his first assignment. He told us how the Knights were so supportive of his ministry among them and welcomed him with open arms. It didn't take long before he became a brother Knight and a chaplain to the Knights of his local council. Then he asked "why is it that the Knights of Columbus love priests?" In other words, why is it that the Knights seek to work closely with priests and to have them become Knights?

The truth is that the Knights of Columbus seek to establish the spirit of collaboration/solidarity between themselves and the Church hierarchy: bishops, priests and deacons. One could say that this may be due to the spirit of their father founder, Fr. Michael McGivney, who was a priest himself. It is not surprising then that the Knights love and support their priests in order to keep the spirit and the vision of their founder alive. The Knights strive to be in close solidarity with the Holy Father, the Pope, their local bishops and the priests. Each council endeavors to have a chaplain, who is always a priest. The Knights see their chaplain as a shepherd and looks up to him for encouragement and guidance, so that their enthusiasm may be duly spiritual and their thinking in congruence with the teaching of the Church and policies of the local bishop and pastors.

A brief history of how it all started will help us to appreciate the wonderful link between the Knights of Columbus and priests. The Knights of Columbus was founded in 1882 by a 29-year-old priest, Father Michael J. McGivney, in the basement of St. Mary's Church in New Haven, Connecticut. Father

McGivney was then the pastor of this parish. As a master dreamer, Fr. McGivney's vision was built around help and service. Initially it was meant to help the orphans and widows. "to set up a parish-based lay organization to help Catholic men remain steadfast to their faith, and offer protection for Catholic families." Providing for the financial security of Catholic families is central in the dream the founder had for the Knights. Today, in keeping with the aim of the founder, the Knights of Columbus are Catholic men dedicated to charity, unity, fraternity, patriotism, and defense of the priesthood.

In the light of the above fact, it can be said that, the Knights of Columbus play an important role in the Church. If I was asked to use one word to describe the function of the Knights for the Catholic Church, I would say "service." Knights are beacons of service. Service and making difference in people's lives are the hallmarks of what they do. So one can say without mincing words that Call to Service is one of the things priests and Knights of Columbus have in common. We are like partners in progress. Many of us priests are proud to associate with the knights. The Knights are committed to assisting and supporting bishops and priests in furthering the work of evangelization in their local churches and councils. Two things that stand out are: the Knights have growing initiative to involve the bishops, priests, and deacons in their councils by making them brother Knights, and growing initiative to the promotion of vocation to the priesthood. For example, through their Vocation Programs, the order supports vocations to the priesthood and religious life. Many seminarians have become priests through the sponsorship of the Knights of Columbus. Many of us priests are proud to be called brother Knights.

CHAPTER III

GOD'S CALL TO DISCIPLESHIP

"God, infinitely perfect and blessed in Himself, in a plan of sheer goodness, freely created man and woman to make them share in His own blessed life." For this reason, at every time and in every place, God draws close to mankind. He calls them to seek Him, to know Him, to love Him with all their strength. He calls together all men and women, scattered and divided by sin, into the unity of his family, the Church.[38]

To accomplish this, when the fullness of time had come, God sent His Son as Redeemer and Savior. In His Son and through Him, He invites human kind to become, in the Holy Spirit, His adopted children and thus heirs of His blessed life.

Jesus Calls

Oddly enough, Jesus Himself chooses and called personally those He asked to follow him.

- Ordinarily, each person decides to follow a master of his or her own choice. In this way, each community, each little group, had its own adherents, each master his own followers. For example, John the Baptist had his own disciples.
- No doubt people asked the master if they could accompany him. But when Jesus calls people, he calls them with authority.

Note, it is not even "join me in following the Lord, in following wisdom, or in following the way . . . " but "follow me!" With that use of the first person singular Christ attracts people to Him with injunction.

And what people marveled at was the extraordinary obedience of those who were called and sent by the Lord. They went without hesitation, without delay. His formula of invitation is "come follow me." They left everything to follow the Master. This was the case with the fishermen-brothers from

---

38   The Catechism of the Catholic Church *Liberia Edirice Vaticana* 1994, No. I

Galilee Simon and Andrew, James and John—who were to become the pillars of the apostolic college. "And immediately they left their nets, father, boat and fish and followed Him."[39]

Each evangelist on his own, reflects in a particular way how the first Christian communities were formed and instructed. He has his own emphasis and his own preferences in these stories of the Apostles being called and taken on. But all are in agreement on the institution by Jesus of a group formed of twelve members, twelve like the twelve tribes of Israel. This is how the new people of God comes to birth, its universal application symbolized by this number. They are at one and the same time companions and ambassadors, disciples and Apostles.

"And He went up into the hills and called to Himself those whom He desired; and they came to Him. And he appointed the twelve, to be with Him, and to be sent out to preach and have authority to cast out demons. Simon whom he surnamed Peter, James, whom He surnamed Barnabas, the sons of thunder, Andrew, and Philip, and Bartholomew, and Matthew and Thomas and James son of Alphaeus, Thaddeus, Simon, Jude and Judas Iscariot, who betrayed Him."[40]

I choose you

The call to discipleship is a divine initiative. Jesus calls and mankind responds. No one can call himself. The reason why Jesus calls is because He did not intend the spreading of the good news to end with Him. So He in turn, called His Apostles, trained them for three years, and sent them out through the power of the Holy Spirit. That is why Christ said, "You did not choose me, but I chose you and appointed you that you should go and bear fruit and that your fruit should abide" (Jn. 15:14).

The Lord only knows how and why He chose some people and rejected some people. For example, you cannot question Jesus why He gave a negative reply to that young man who wanted to follow him, as St Luke writes: "I will follow you wherever you go" (Lk. 9:57-62). Jesus replied: "Foxes have holes and the birds of the air have nests, but the Son of man has nowhere to lay his head."[41]

---

39   Mk. 1:16-18, Mtt. 4:18, Lk. 5:1-11, Jn. 1:35-45
40   Mk. 3:13-19
41   Lk. 9:57-58

On the contrary, when the Lord calls one, His call is always magisterial, that is with authority. He doesn't seek your opinion whether you will like it or not. Look at the call of the Apostles, Paul of the New Testament, Gideon, Moses, Jeremiah, etc. The Lord will give a solution to your excuse to shy away from the mission of the call.

In everything He did, Jesus knew He was inspired and sustained by the Spirit of God. It is moreover His very identity: in calling Him Christ in Greek or Mashiah (Messiah) in Hebrew, He has been labeled as the one who had received the anointing of the Spirit, the one on whom the Spirit of God rested. In this way, He was able to proclaim in the synagogue at Nazareth, "The Spirit of the Lord is upon me, because He has anointed me to preach good news to the poor. He has sent me. . . ." (Lk. 4:18, quoting Isaiah 61:1). Those whom Jesus in turn has chosen to continue His work are not just "Christian" in the sense in which one talks about Kantians, Gaullists, or Marxists to describe the heirs of Kant, de Gaulle, or Marx. Having received the Spirit of Christ, they are themselves like the other Christs, and each of them can say in his turn: "The spirit of the Lord is upon me. He has sent me. . . ."[42]

Discipleship means learning the mater's style/skills

A master teaches the way a father teaches, by sharing the task. A father teaches His child by saying, "Son, come, help me with this job."

A short story may be of help here. One day, I paid a visit to my carpenter friend, Jemmy, in his workshop. I met him with this boy, Tony, who was learning the master's style.

The master chose a moment to say to his boy: "Tony, I need your help. Drive in this next nail for me." The boy hit the nail, bending it over. The father pulled out the nail and started another, but the boy bents that one too. Hammering in the next nail a little further, the father explains, "Now, son, hold the hammer a little shorter and keep your eye right on the nail." Taught in this way, the son finally had confidence and drove the nail solidly into the board. His father then turned to him and said with a smile and a tone of real pride, "Thanks a lot Tony, you are a big help to your Dad."[43]

In reality, who was being helped? Tony's father could have driven that nail into the board more quickly and easily himself, but he was more

---

42   Tom Forrest, New Evangelization 2000 Magazine Vol. 23. 1994, p. 15
43   Ibid. p. 10

interested in giving a useful lesson/skill to his son. In the same way, Jesus our Master, could save the world more easily without us. Unburdened by our weakness and infidelity, He could position the stars of heaven to spell out the words, Jesus Christ is Lord! He could send legions of angels to obliterate every center of opposition and instrument of evil on earth. But Jesus desires to teach us how to love. So he says to us, "Come help me with my mission of love; help to save the world!"

As our understanding of the master/disciple relationship grows, it becomes impossible to claim to be Christ's disciple if we do not spend time in His presence, if we talk with everyone who calls on the telephone, and stop to chat with someone we meet on the street, but still don't have time to speak daily with Jesus in prayer. Our claim to discipleship is hollow.

Talking and listening to the master is the first priority of a disciple. Similarly, if we have time to watch the news on television and read the newspaper, but claim to have no time for reading and studying the life of Jesus in the Gospels, our claim to discipleship is false. True disciples know that the Good News is found in the pages of Scriptures, and they make sure they have the time to go there.

Entrusted with a mission

And Jesus sent them out on a mission, just as He Himself presented Himself as the one sent by the Father. They too were to proclaim that the kingdom of God was at hand, and they had to bear witness to this by the same actions as Jesus: healing the sick, cleansing lepers, expelling demons and victories over evil in all its forms. And they too would be treated like their Master; hatred and persecution were waiting for them. That formed part of their witness.[44]

There is nothing optional about this final command of Jesus. We must go into action immediately. We are to transform people into committed disciples of the Redeemer, targeting not just a few individuals but every nation, race, and culture on earth.

We must carry Christ's teaching in all its fullness to the very ends of the earth, and our success is guaranteed because Jesus is with us every step of the way.

---

44   Lk. 10:1-10

Vocation discernment for priesthood as a call to discipleship.

Vocation discernment can be seen as emanating from feelings, spiritual movements, motivations and spiritual indicators going on within and around someone and taking a step forward to determine if he has a divine calling to the priesthood or religious life.

One cannot be experiencing vocation discernment without a master in the picture: call him a spiritual director, vocation director, pastor, or teacher, etc.—that is to say, someone more spiritually experienced to guide you in the discernment process.

A typical example of vocation discernment is found in the biblical story of Samuel and his master Eli. Here, Samuel was asleep in his usual place, in the temple of the Lord where the ark of God was. There and then the Lord called Samuel. When Samuel answered "Here I am," he ran to Eli, thinking that he was the one that called him. Eli asked him to go back to sleep as he did not call him. So he did. Again the Lord called him a second time. He answered, "Here I am," and went back to Eli saying, "You called me," and Samuel again asked him to go back to sleep. After the third call, Eli discerned that it was the Lord who was calling the young man. So he asked him to go back to sleep and to respond "Speak Lord your servant is listening" if he was called again.

When Samuel went back to sleep in his place, the Lord came and revealed his presence, calling out to Samuel as before, "Samuel Samuel." Samuel answered, "Speak Lord, for your servant is listening." The Lord then spoke to Samuel and made known His plans for him and the people of Israel. Then Samuel became an "accredited prophet of the Lord.[45]

To help someone discern if he has a vocation to the priesthood is a long process. As the saying goes, "Rome was not built in a day." So also a priest is not born overnight. It is a lengthy and rigorous but rewarding process. Houses of discernment, seminaries, and on a grass root level: parishes, and homes are breeding grounds and conducive environments where God's calling continues to grow until one takes up the responsibility of saying yes. This yes is a free response to God's voice. The person in discernment should be close to our Lord, to the Church and to the sacraments; especially the Eucharist. He has to remain focused under the auspices of a master (competent authority).

---

45   Lk. 9:62

Hearing God's call "means learning to keep our gaze fixed on Jesus, growing close to Him, listening to His word and encountering Him in the sacraments; it means learning to conform our will to His,"[46] Said Our Holy Father, Pope Benedict XVI.

The period of discernment can be considered as being from the moment of first inquiry, through the time of studies at the seminary, till the day of the laying on of hands (ordination). It is a precarious period, a period of searching and determining the divine will in one's life. Messing with this important moment is like playing with fire. One is in a very important process of apprenticeship, just like the Apostles who remained under the direction of the Lord Jesus for three years from the time they heard Him say "come follow me."

At some point every Catholic boy should stop and ask himself, "is God calling me?" God's call to the priesthood is an intricate reality that moves like a wave or a tide. It comes and goes, and then persists that one may not avoid it at that point even after ignoring it for a long time. It is never too late to answer God's call in so far as you are still unmarried and are of canonical age. Some hear the voice early in life and then begin the process of discernment, and some hear it much later in their adult life. Each priest has a story of his vocation at the tip of his fingers.

Here is the list of common vocation indicators that might be termed as God's calling to consider priesthood.

Check list for Divine calling to the Priesthood:

1. Do you have a growing longing for things of God?

2. Do you have developing love for Jesus Christ, for the Church and for priests?

3. Do you have a growing love to the Eucharist and the Mass?

4. Do you enjoy seeing a priest say Mass and desire to be the one saying the Mass?

---

46   Sam. 3:1-18

5. Do you enjoy having religious discussions with friends or family?

6. Are you excited to go to Church or attending religious functions and gatherings?

7. Do you desire strongly to help others, especially those in need?

8. Do you like to serve other people including family members?

9. Has someone including your parents or family members, fellow Christians encouraged you to become a priest or asked you if you will like to be a priest?

10. Has someone told you that you look like a priest?

11. Do people remark that you are different, because of your attachment to spiritual values?

12. Do you enjoy praying a lot? Do you feel yourself spiritually connected to God?

If you have one or more of these, it may well be a sign of God's call to become a priest. Do not suppress it. Your first step is that you may want to talk to your pastor or the diocesan vocation director to help you process the spiritual movement going on inside of you. Feeling God's call requires a free response.

Obstacle to the call of Christ

Here it is important to remark that the major obstacle to hearing the call of Christ to the priesthood is the world and the worldly allurement engendered by the evil one. This assertion can be exemplified by the experience of Jesus in the Gospel of Luke, where Jesus called a man to follow him, but he answered, "Let me go back now, for first I want to bury my father."[47] One can see immediately how this man presented a problem to excuse himself, the statement, first I want to bury my father, perhaps may mean that he should bury his father who has just died. But most probably it means that he

---

47   http://www.ncregister.com/blog/edward-pentin/benedict-xvi-on-fosstering-vocations#ixzz1sSdZ2X28. The Holy Father made the appeal in his message for the 48th World Day of Prayer for Vocations, released by the Vatican today. The day takes place on 15th May 2011 on the Theme "Proposing Vocations in the Local Church." Read more: http://www.ncregister.com/blog/edward-pentin/benedict-xvi-on-fosstering-vocations#ixzz1sSgXnvJW

wanted to look after his aged father up to the time of burial before following Jesus.

Another who was also called by Jesus said, "I will follow you Lord, but first let me go ad say goodbye to my family, to him Jesus said, whoever has put his hand to the plow and looks back is not fit for the kingdom of God."[48] From all these, it must be concluded that when a call from Jesus reaches you, it is the complete will of God for you in this precise moment. One is expected to leave everything, including your excuses, your duties: perhaps these would be duties only in a world of the dead. Perhaps other people will attend to that need including the angels.

Cost of discipleship

A way to meditate on the full calling that a true disciple has from Jesus is to prayerfully study chapter 8 of the Gospel of Saint Mark. Here Jesus said to his disciples, "Whoever wishes to come after me must deny himself, take up his cross and follow me. For whoever wishes to save his life will lose it. But whoever loses his life for my sake and that of the Gospel will save it"(Mk 8:34-35). From the above reference of the Bible, Jesus teaches us the necessity of losing oneself. Examples abound in the Bible of those who lost themselves for the sake of God. For example, this means to lose oneself like Abraham, who went to a strange land away from his home.[49] It means to lose oneself like Moses, who agreed to be the leader of an oppressed people.[50] It also means to lose oneself like St Paul, who was beheaded for the sake of the Gospel. It means to rid oneself of this temporary existence so as to be reborn of God, like Ignatius the Martyr. Condemned to be eaten by lions, he said, "I am the wheat of God; may I be ground by the teeth of wild animals to be converted into the pure bread of Christ." By these words, "take up your cross and follow me," Jesus teaches us the best way to follow His footsteps as the Master. We must follow His path to His own cross if we want to gain and participate in His glory. This reminds me of the popular adage that "there is no crown without a cross." We take our cross by accepting freely the sacrifices that the Father sends each day, We receive from now on something more marvelous than what was sacrificed: inner freedom and more profound happiness.[51]

---

48   Lk. 9:57
49   Cf. Gen. 12:1-6
50   Cf. Ex. 3:16-17
51   Cf. Mt. 10:30

Jesus spells out in detail all that is involved in following Him. But before facing all the challenges of our Lord's instructions, it is important first of all to study the value and importance of becoming true disciples, and make certain that we have set it as our own priority.

We can learn about priorities by taking a final look at the story of Elijah and Elisha. We read in the Second Book of Kings that after Elijah struck and parted the waters of the Jordan with his cloak, he turned and said to Elisha, "Make your request. What can I do for you before I am taken from you?" Elijah's desire to console with these words again reflects his warm relationship with Elisha, but it is more important to note the response of his disciple. Elisha asks his departing master, "Let me inherit a double share of your spirit." His master replies, "Your request is a difficult one, but if you see me while I am being taken from you, it shall be as you ask."

We know that Elisha did see Elijah carried up to heaven by a whirlwind and a fiery chariot, proof that his request had been granted. Elisha then walked to the Jordan and with a double blow of his cloak parted the waters just as Elijah had done before him. When the prophets of Jericho saw that Elisha was able to work the same wonders his master had worked, they cried out in admiration, "Truly the spirit of Elijah has come to rest on Elisha."[52]

Jesus, our Master, has said to us the same thing that the master of Elisha said to Him. He has said it often and unconditionally: "Ask me whatever you wish and it shall be given to you."[53] Our own priorities are revealed in what we choose to ask: good health, good salary, good home, second car in the garage, solutions to personal problems, or other human comforts. There is nothing wrong with asking for these good things. But if we learn from the example of Elisha and his master and hear just what Jesus explicitly and repeatedly promises us as his parting gift, the very first thing we will request is "Lord, enrich me with a double share of your very own spirit."

To have that spirit is to really have the life of Jesus, and that life is the first goal of every true disciple, so wonderful that it makes all else unnecessary.[54] When we make this our first cry, Christ proves faithful to His word; His spirit comes upon us, and we are empowered to work Christ's own works and even greater ones.[55] Then others looking at us can say, "Truly the spirit of Jesus has come to rest on him." When this happens, Christ again has a Body, and Christ again becomes visible in us, his disciples.

---

52   2 Kings 2:7-15
53   Mtt. 18:19, 7:1-11; 21:22; Mk. 11:23, Jn. 14:12-14
54   Phil. 3:18
55   Phil. 3:18

The master speaks with authority

Jesus sent two disciples, saying to them, "Go into the village opposite you, and immediately you will find an ass tethered, and a colt with her. Untie them and bring them here to me. . . . The disciples went and did as Jesus had ordered them.[56]

"The disciples approached Jesus and said, 'Where do you want us to prepare for you to eat the Passover?' He said, 'Go into the city to a certain man and tell him, The teacher says, My appointed time draws near; in your house I shall celebrate the Passover with my disciples.' The disciples then did as Jesus had ordered, and prepared the Passover."[57]

He leads his disciples to pray

"He was praying in a certain place, and when He had finished, one of his disciples said to Him, 'Lord, teach us to pray just as John taught his disciples.' He said to them, 'When you pray, say: Father, hallowed be your name, your kingdom come. Give us each day our daily bread and forgive us our sins for we ourselves forgive everyone in debt to us.'"[58]

In this mode of prayer Jesus instructs and authorizes his disciples to address God as "Father," using the very title that He Himself employed in His prayer of praise. It can be observed that this prayer is divided into two parts. The first part brings praises unto God, and the second part is petition. With his prayer Jesus teaches us how to pray. In this, Our Lord's prayer, we find that after praise or thanksgiving, the community is to request the "Father" to sustain it in its daily need of food, to entreat His forgiveness for sin, and to beg Him not to be confronted with temptation to apostasy. The second petition has an explicative dimension: The disciples state their own attitude of forgiveness toward all who wrong them. All these petitions thus express a humble confidence and reliance, but also a conviction that they be heard.

"He went, as was His custom, to the Mount of Olives, and the disciples followed Him. When He arrived at the place He said to them, 'pray that you may not undergo the test.' After withdrawing about a stone's throw from them and kneeling, He prayed, saying, 'Father, if you are willing, take this cup away from me; still, not my will but yours be done. . . .' Then he arose

---

56   Mt. 21:2-3, 6
57   Mt. 26:17-19
58   Lk. 11:1-4

from prayer and came to his disciples, only to find them asleep exhausted with grief. He said to them, 'Why are you sleeping? Wake up and pray.'"[59]

Women share in discipleship

"Mary . . . bent over into the tomb and saw two angels in white sitting there, one at the head and one at the feet where the body of Jesus had been. And they said to her, 'Woman, why are you weeping?' She said to them, 'They have taken my Lord, and I don't know where they laid him.' When she had said this, she turned around and saw Jesus there, but did not know it was Jesus. Jesus said to her, 'Women, why are you weeping? Whom are you looking for?' She thought it was the gardener and said to Him, 'Sir, if you carried him away, tell me where you laid him, and I will take him.' Jesus said to her, 'Mary!' She turned and said to him in Hebrew, "Rabbouni,' which means Teacher. . . . Mary of Magdala went and announced to the disciples, 'I have seen the Lord.'"[60]

"In Joppa there was a disciple named Tabitha. . . . She was completely occupied with good deeds and almsgiving. Now during those days she fell sick and died, so after washing her, they laid her out in a room upstairs. When (Peter) arrived, they took him to the room upstairs where all the widows came to him weeping and showing him the tunics and cloaks that Dorcas had made while she was with them. Peter sent them all out and knelt down and prayed. Then he turned to her body and said, 'Tabitha, rise up.' She opened her eyes, saw Peter, and sat up. He gave her his hand and raised her up, and when he had called the holy ones and the widows, he presented her alive."[61]

---

59   Lk. 22:39-46
60   Jn. 20:11-16, 18
61   Acts 9:36, 39-41

CHAPTER IV

PROGRESS IN HOLINESS

From time to time we should examine ourselves for signs of spiritual growth, seeing what fruits of conversion and holiness we can discover. It is true that the Lord himself remains the final judge[62] but such examinations can indicate whether we are making progress, and what steps should be taken to cooperate better with the abundant grace of God.

Our progress in holiness should be leaving visible traces, signs exhibiting the intensity of the divine life in us. The faithful should be able to see Christ walking, praying, teaching, sanctifying, and healing within us. We should, in other words, be an on-going epiphany of the good shepherd and tend His flock throughout the ages.

St. Paul gives us a list of the "Fruits of the Holy Spirit" that manifest our inner holiness and reveal the presence of the Holy Spirit who "gives witness with our spirit that we are children of God."[63] Love, joy, peace, patience, kindness, goodness, faithfulness, gentleness and self-control are the fruits St. Paul listed. We should not look at this list abstractly, but rather study it very practically to see how each of these fruits gives concrete direction to our daily living.

Priestly love should reflect Christ's love by being a total giving. A priest lives not to be filled, but in order to fill others. It is enough for him that he is already filled with Christ: "The life I live now is not my own; Christ is living in me."[64] The priest is wedded to the church, and as St. Paul reminds us, any second marriage would only be a distraction from his sublime calling. "The unmarried man is busy with the Lord's affairs, concerned with pleasing the Lord; but the married man is busy with this world's demands and occupied with pleasing his wife. This means he is divided."[65] For this reason, our priestly celibacy requires abstinence not only from carnal gratification, but also from any emotional connections that tend to divide our hearts.

Every state of life produces its own special happiness, but priestly joy anticipates the joy of heaven in a very special way. It is the joy of a wisdom

---

62   Cf. I Cor. 4:4
63   Rom. 8:16
64   Gal. 2:20
65   I Cor. 7:32-33

that lets us see everything through the prism of God, our Creator. It is the joy of a faith and hope that blocks our despair and depression. Wasn't it this kind of joy in some priests we knew in our youth that led us to the priesthood? Without wanting to oversimplify, wouldn't vocations again be on the increase if we were inspiring today's youth by letting them see the joy we find in the life we have chosen and for which we were chosen by God?

We have peace when our own house is set in order with God. And once we have this peace, we can communicate it to others. I encourage you, dear brother priests, to stay available to those wishing to make peace with God by remaining faithful to the confessional. Make it as easy as possible for people to confess their guilt, but do not become a scandal by changing Christian morality with your own say-so. Do not set up schedules for the sacraments that fit your own convenience, but try to meet the needs of the people in the circumstances of their busy lives. For example, in areas where communion may be received either kneeling or standing, give the personal freedom of choice the Church allows.

The kindness of a priest

The kindness of a priest is shown by his generous use of time and by the way he speaks to others. He does not frighten people by growling when they call on the phone. For children he has a smile and words of encouragement, and even has time to listen patiently to the parish bore, drop a note to someone suffering, or fill in for another priest when the need arises. How important it is for people and for our brother priests to see in us these fruits of kindness!

Goodness of a priest

Although goodness is similar to kindness, it goes far deeper. It leads us to act as Christ would act in all circumstances of life. People judge a priest to be 'good,' when they see that his priesthood is his whole life. He is not esteemed when he gives the impression that being a priest for him is no more than an eight-hour-a-day profession. People consider him a good priest when he dresses as a priest, prays as a priest, is available to them as their priest, enriches the parishioners and not himself by preparing his sermons, and finds a diversity of ways to serve their spiritual needs. Good priests also stay faithful to their daily Mass and recitation of the Liturgy of the Hours. False arguments of certain modern writers have misled some, but good priests never neglect these aspects of the easy yoke and sweet burden of Christ.[66]

The Faithfulness of a Priest

Regarding the fruit of faithfulness, I believe that many priests today are striving to be faithful. The important question is to whom? Today so many claim to be speaking for Christ, and yet so few are in agreement with each other. Some claim fidelity to truths they question by saying they only take exception to how they are expressed. Some claim fidelity to the Magisterium, but sometimes the pencil wants to move the hand. False arguments of certain modern writers have misled some, and some theologians set themselves against their bishops. Our fidelity should be directed towards the universal Magisterium of the Church of Christ. Faithfulness is a gift from Christ given to protect us from exactly the kind of confusion and rebellion we are experiencing today. A simple phrase from Lumen Gentium makes it clear to whom we should direct our fidelity. It tells us that even "the college or body of bishops has . . . no authority unless united with the Roman Pontiff, Peter's successor."[67] A priest is not faithful to the teaching of the Church if he is not faithful and obedient to his bishop.

> *Good priests also stay faithful to their daily mass and recitation of the liturgy of the hours. False arguments of certain modern writers have misled some, but good priests never neglect these aspects of the easy yoke and sweet burden of Christ.*

---

66   Cf. Mtt. 11:30
67   Cf. Lumen Gentium No. 22

The gentleness of a priest

In prophesying the gentleness of the Messiah, Isaiah said, "A bruised reed he shall not break." What a graphic image! Something as fragile as a reed, a bruised reed at that, and yet Christ will not break it.

We priests are called to practice the gentleness of Christ by the way we help people of different categories and people of various needs. In the Lord, we are brothers and sisters. For example, as priest chaplains or pastors, we visit those who are suffering with human weakness: illness, mental, or economic challenges. The first reaction on the part of the priest is pastoral care for this person/persons in need.

How about priests ministering to young women who wish to give their lives to Christ, but find that upon admission they too must choose to carry one of the banners of internal political dispute, so destructive to community life. Coming to mind also are parents who at great expense send their child to Catholic school only to discover that the instruction given is at odds with authentic Catholic tradition. Again my mind flashes to a mother in this permissive age, torn between the need to discipline her child and the fear of setting him against her or fear that he will run away from the house. My brother priests, again I say, be gentle to all these people who are deeply afflicted. Never compromise the teaching of Christ, but always be conscious of what is being suffered, and deal with people gently and with great sensitivity to their needs.

The self-control of a priest

People expect priests to be men of self-control, men of moderation. We should have control of our tempers and our appetites, living with a restraint that saves us from having reputations as fashion plates and gourmets. Before acting, we should think about the effect the things we say and do might have upon others, especially the weak. "All things are lawful, but not all things are helpful," as St. Paul tells us.[68] Many will know Christ only by the way they see us acting, and we could easily mislead them if we fail to keep control of our emotions and appetites.

These fruits of the Holy Spirit give flesh to our spiritual life, since they are concrete manifestations in daily living of our inner holiness. Only by

---

68   I Cor. 10:23 R.S.V.

examining how our internal spiritual life is manifested in the things we say and do can we judge where we need further growth in priestly holiness.

With these fruits of individual holiness, all priests must join together to be for the world a more powerful, more universal, and more effective manifestation of Christ, our only High Priest. He is the fruit of Mary's womb, and He must be the fruit of our generous priestly lives as well. We must respond faithfully to His call to holiness, "so that in our bodies the life of Jesus may also be revealed."[69]

---

69   I Cor. 4:10, 11 Cor. 4:10

CHAPTER V

HOLINESS OF LIFE, CALL TO HOLINESS, AND PRIESTLY OBEDIENCE

Obedience is a priestly value/virtue of primary importance. Here, the priest must always be ready to seek not his own will, but the will of Him who sent him.[70]

Holiness and priestly obedience

The fundamental reason for the priest's obedience is the fact that he is a personal instrument of Christ and therefore should conform himself totally to Him. Christ, "although He was Son, He learned to obey through suffering."[71] "He emptied himself to assume the condition of a slave," becoming obedient even to accepting death,[72] and through His obedience He cancelled the disobedience of Adam and earned the salvation for all.[73]

The very sacrifice of Christ on the Cross acquired salvific value and significance through His obedience and His fidelity to the will of the Father. It could be said, then, that obedience to the Father is the very heart of the priesthood of Christ.

Like Christ's obedience, the priest's obedience expresses the will of God which is made manifest to the priest through his legitimate superiors. This availability must be understood as a true act of personal freedom, the result of a choice continually deepened in the presence of God in prayer.

The virtue of obedience, intrinsically required by the Sacrament of Holy Orders and by the hierarchical structure of the Church, is clearly promised by the clergy, first in the rite of diaconal ordination, and then in priestly ordination. With it the priest strengthens his will of submission, thus participating in the dynamics of the obedience of Christ made servant, obedient till death on the Cross.[74]

---

70   Cf. Jn. 4:34, 5:30, 6:38
71   Heb. 5:18
72   Ph. 2:7-8
73   Rom. 5:19
74   Phil. 2:7-8

In contemporary culture, the value of the individual's subjectivity and autonomy is emphasized, as if intrinsic to one's dignity. This value, in itself positive, if made absolute and claimed outside of its just context, assumes a negative value. This attitude could also be manifested in ecclesial circles, and in the very life of the priest whenever his activities in the service of the community become reduced to a subjective realm.

In reality, the priest, by the very nature of his ministry, is at the service of Christ and the Church. Therefore, he must be disposed to accept all that is justly indicated by his superiors and, in a particular way, if not legitimately impeded, must accept and faithfully fulfill the task entrusted to him by his ordinary.

The priest's obedience is ecclesial, linked with his own ordination, because his mission cannot be realized except in union with the hierarchy. Therefore, pastoral love demands that priests "dedicate their own wills through obedience to the service of God and their brothers." This love requires that they accept and carry out in a spirit of faith whatever is commanded or recommended by the sovereign pontiff, their own bishop, or other superiors.

Obedience for a priest is first of all a habitual disposition of mind, which links him with the will of God through the authority of his superiors. It enables him to overcome the earthly concept of the autonomy of the person; and this entails a faithful execution of the norms, with recognition of his place in the Presbyteriate and of his duty of service in the hierarchy.[75]

The areas in which priestly obedience should show itself specifically today are:

i   Fidelity to the Magisterium
ii   Acceptance of appointments
iii   Observance of the requirement and norms of Liturgy etc.
iv   Unity in pastoral planning

Fidelity to the Magisterium
Based on his Christian and priestly identity, this fidelity should express itself concretely in an attitude of obedience to the teaching authority of both the Roman Pontiff and the bishops. Priests should not deviate from magisterial teachings and follow unapproved theories or personal convictions. Such

---

75   Opt. Cit. p. 60 Directory

fidelity is indispensable for their own authenticity and for them to be able to offer their faithful a teaching conformed to revealed truth; the pastor should guide his flock with sound doctrine and should not disturb it with uncertain or deviant theories.[76]

Acceptance of appointments

The priest's fidelity to his task as evangelizer and pastor should be seen in his readiness to accept and fulfill whatever mission is entrusted to him by his bishop. In Vatican II, collaborative action of the priest refers to him as coworker with the order of bishops.[77] A spirit of faith and obedience is needed for this, with an attitude of availability; not asking insistently to be assigned to certain tasks or parishes, or refusing the task assigned by the bishop. When appointments are being made, priests should be open with the bishop, expressing their idea in sincere and frank dialogue, but once a decision has been made, they should accept it joyfully, without further objections. Even if at times they find that they are not very suitable for a task accepted in obedience, they should not forget that it is the duty of diocesan priests, as collaborators of the bishop, to give themselves fully, to try to provide for the needs of the diocese. When they reach retirement age, they should hand in their resignation to the bishop and be willing to leave their post.[78]

Observance of the requirements and norms of their function

Pastoral service in a Christian community, especially in the case of a parish, requires priests to be regular and faithful in their conduct. In what concerns Mass intentions, the Church has laid down regulations for these in the new Code of Canon Law, and priests should follow them carefully and objectively. There should be no impression of financial interest conveyed, and one should be prepared to offer Mass without a stipend, especially for the poor. General and diocesan rules concerning combination and the Mass for the people should be observed. Every stipend received, the date of celebration, the intention specified, the fulfillment of the obligation, and the transfer of intentions to other celebrants should be properly recorded. In parishes there should be a special register for Mass intentions.

---

76   2 Tim. 2:14, Tit. 2:1
77   Cf. OP 2
78   Ibid p. 60

The parish registers for baptisms, marriages, deaths and other items prescribed by the Episcopal Conference and the bishop are important for the proper exercises of the rights and duties of the faithful. The pastor should see to it that they are properly kept. In every parish there should be safely maintained archives, including the parish registers, letters from the bishop, and other important documents.

Priests should wear clerical dress in accordance with the norms of the Episcopal Conference and legitimate custom. They should not lightly give up this sign of their state, which can be both a safeguard for themselves and a positive witness to the faithful.

Residence in their parish is a duty imposed on pastors by the terms of their service. However, in accordance with the directives of their bishop, priests need and have a right to a suitable period of vacation each year, for physical and spiritual restoration. They should also try to take a weekly break for recreation and for useful reading. Before leaving the parish for a long period, however, they should arrange with the bishop for someone to take their place.

Call to holiness and priestly chastity in celibate life

Celibacy, in fact, is a gift which the Church has received and desires to retain, convinced that it is good for the Church itself and for the world.

Like any evangelical value, consecrated celibacy should be seen as that liberating novelty which the world, especially today, demands as a radical testimony that following Christ is a sign of the eschatological reality. "Not all can understand it, but only those to whom it has been given. For there were eunuchs who were born from their mothers' womb, and there are eunuchs who were made so by man, and there are eunuchs who have made themselves eunuchs for the sake of the kingdom of heaven. He that can understand, let him understand."[79]

To live with love and generosity and the gift received, it is particularly important that the priest understand, from the beginning of his seminary formation the theological and spiritual motives for the ecclesiastical discipline of celibacy. This particular gift of God demands the observance of chastity, the perfect and perpetual continence for the Kingdom of Heaven

---

79   Mtt. 19:10-12

so sacred ministers can more easily adhere to Christ with an undivided heart and dedicate themselves more freely to the service of God and man.

In today's often permissive society, priests are called upon to reconfirm their vocation to perfect continence in celibacy, through which they are consecrated to God in a new and distinguished way. They more easily hold fast to Him with undivided heart[80] and are dedicated to the service of their brothers and sisters with greater liberty and effectiveness, receiving the gifts of a greater "paternity in Christ."[81]

Chastity should not be considered a law that inhibits personal growth; rather its positive aspects should be stressed.

Perfect chastity in celibacy is first of all a grace that the Father grants to those who pray for it with perseverance, truth, and humility. However, ordination does not protect them from every temptation and danger, and chastity for the kingdom is not something that can be acquired once and for all but is the result of a daily conquest. Priests should take the normal means and not neglect practices of proven efficacy.

Here are some practical guidelines to help priests maintain perpetual continence (celibacy) for the Kingdom of Heaven.

Sincerity with God and with oneself

First of all, they should have the courage to be sincere with God and with their own conscience, looking frankly at their aspirations, difficulties, and weaknesses. Self-knowledge helps one pick out the points to be strengthened and those to correct; sincerity with God guarantees supernatural help and strengthens one's confidence and joy in the priesthood.

Use of the normal means

Experience indicates the need to make use of both supernatural and natural means in order to be faithful to celibacy. Thus, priests should renew every day their total dedication to Christ; they should ask in prayer for the gift of fidelity and perseverance; they should entrust their heart to Mary, Queen of Virgins; and they should have recourse to mortification, which increases self-control and helps overcome obstacles.[82]

---

80   Cf. I Cor. 7:32-34
81   *Presbyterium Ordinis* 16
82   Decree on the Ministry and Life of Priests *(Presbyterium Ordinis)* Vol. II 1965, No. 17 p. 896

Human maturity is an indispensable premise for a life of priestly chastity. Priests should have control of their affective life, and, if necessary should seek expert help, preferably from priests, they should have friendships with other priests. They should be happy to live in common unity with them, avoiding isolation for too long a time They should not expose themselves needlessly to danger, they should be moderate in their use of food, and especially in their use of alcohol and tobacco. They should be prudent in their reading, the shows they attend, their use of audiovisual media, and their choice of entertainment.

They should realize that at times celibacy contrasts with family or ethnic structures. Even in these cases, they should be faithful to their undertaking, explaining to their people, by word but especially by their lives, the true meaning of their choice.

Conduct with women

In their relations with women, special care should be taken because of the priestly state and the danger of scandalizing the faithful. This holds particularly for nuns, who are closer to priests through their religious spirit, apostolic ideal, and way of life. Priests, therefore, while they have a duty to have good relations with all women and to involve them in the apostolate, should avoid preferential attentions and anything that might create special bonds and diminish freedom of heart. Taking account of local culture, they should avoid all conduct that might disturb the faithful and diminish the credibility of the priesthood, such as being alone with a woman for a considerable time, admitting women to private rooms, giving them presents, traveling alone with them, etc. In this whole matter, it is not enough that the priest himself should know that he is not guilty of anything; he should also follow the criterion of St. Paul: "For our part, we avoid giving scandal to anyone, so that our ministry may not be brought into discredit."[83]

As for women employed in the priest's house, the regulations of the Bishop and of the Episcopal Conference should be observed.

---

83   2 Cor 6:3, 8:31

Relations with one's relatives

Relations with his family are important for a priest, as he should find in his family a natural support for his life. In certain cultures, the problem of a priest's relations with his family can become acute, involving not only the human and relational aspect but also finances and justice. An evangelical attitude must be adopted, which will enable him to live in common with his family and to help them, without losing his freedom for the ministry.

Christian families should be educated to look upon a priestly vocation as a gift from God to the community, and to try to share the priest's apostolic ideal without interfering in his priestly task. On the financial side, priests should gratefully try to help their relatives, and especially their parents when in need, but always with discretion and without using Church property. They should never involve their relatives in the administration of Church property. While exercising normal hospitality towards their relatives, they should avoid having them on a permanent basis in their residences, especially if it is a question of groups, and they should see to it that their visits do not interfere with apostolic activity by their frequency and length.

Call to priestly holiness and spirit of poverty

The poverty of Christ has a salvific scope. Christ being rich, became poor for us, that by his poverty we might become rich.[84]

The letter to the Philippians reveals the rapport between the giving of oneself and the spirit of service which enliven the pastoral ministry. St. Paul says that Jesus did not consider "being equal to God a thing to be clung to, but emptied himself, taking a nature of a slave."[85] A priest could hardly be a true servant and minister of his brothers if he were exclusively worried about his comfort and well-being.

The example of Christ would lead the priest to conform himself to Him, with an interior detachment to the goods and riches of the world.[86] The Church is called to follow the road taken by Jesus, who "carried out the work of redemption in poverty and under oppression.[87] Consistency in evangelical poverty and in the preferential option for the poor is indispensable if the ecclesial community, and its pastors are to be credible to the world.

---

84   Cf. 2 Cor. 8:9
85   Phil. 2:6-7
86   Vatican II: No. 12
87   Cf. Phi. 2:6-7; I Cor. 8:9

Priests, by their ordination, "are invited to embrace voluntary poverty. By which they will be more clearly likened to Christ, and will become more devoted to the sacred ministry."

The virtue of poverty for priests is, above all, a total choice of the Lord as their "portion and inhereitance,"[88] it means living in the world without belonging to it[89] and without becoming engrossed in it;[90] it means maintaining a certain freedom and detachment from earthly realities.

Affective and effective poverty and the virtue of justice may also be involved.

A certain financial security is necessary for priests, as those serving at the altar,[91] so that they may exercise their ministry without excessive preoccupation or distraction. The traditional principal holds that the support of their priests is the responsibility of the different Christian communities. It is for the Episcopal Conferences and the individual bishops to decide the best means to ensure a fair remuneration for priests, and to determine what goes to the priest personally and what to the Church. But even the use of personal money should be guided by a spirit of poverty and charity. Priests, therefore, should have the spirituality of pilgrims: What exceeds their own needs should be used for the Church and for works of charity, without accumulating for themselves, in the conviction that the clerical state should not be a means for improving one's own financial situation.

A sober lifestyle

Grateful to divine providence, priests should make use of temporal goods to maintain a worthy but simple lifestyle, with detachment from riches and from anything that might smack of vanity. In this way they will be credible witnesses and be listened to by their people when they speak about the Christian view of temporal goods and their use.

In certain contexts, becoming a priest means moving up on the social ladder. This fact, although involuntary, should not result in the priest being distanced from his own people. His lifestyle, therefore, should be an evangelical witness and should not separate him from the poor; he should be sparing in his use of money, saving so as to be able to help the needy. He should do some chores, gardening etc., without devoting too much

88   Num. 18:20
89   Cf. Jn. 17:14-16
90   Cf. I Cor. 7:31
91   Cf. I Cor. 9:13

time to it at the expense of pastoral work. He should willingly do without what is unnecessary and especially superfluous; he should be frugal in his household arrangements, furniture, clothing, means of transport, audiovisual equipment etc. He should avoid frequent and costly outings and vacations; he should be hardworking and make good use of his time. All of this is required by the spirit of poverty to enable him to approach the poor without humiliating them.

Responsible administration

Aware that the goods of the parish belong to the Church and are not his own, the priest should see that the goods are administered with justice and order, in conformity with their proper ends, which are: the promotion of worship and the apostolate, the honest support of the pastors, and aid to the needy. He should maintain a clear separation, in accordance with diocesan norms, between personal property and that of third parties, such as relatives and friends. In the administration of parish property or that of pastoral works, the help of lay experts should be called upon. A council for financial affairs should be set up, the community should be informed of the financial situation of the parish, prudently but in a spirit of openness, and clear balance sheets should be drawn up in accordance with the bishop's directives.

Financial self-reliance, requests for aid

From a financial point of view, the aim of any Christian community should be self-reliance. Priests should encourage the faithful to provide for the needs of the Church and to give alms. Priest, however, should be discreet in requesting offerings and donation, and these should always be used in conformity with the wishes of the donors; when a specific use is not indicated, they should be used for the needs of the Church and of the poor. Prudence should be taken in requesting, or even in merely accepting, donations from the rich and powerful, so as to be free from possibly dangerous obligation in the ministry.

Attitude to Insurance for illness and old age

As regards this, priests should pay their contributions, according to the law, to civil insurance and pension plans, so that they will be provided for in cases of illness, infirmity, and old age. Where the State does not make adequate provision, the local Churches should themselves set up insurance and pension plans, at the diocesan level or, better, at the level of the Episcopal Conference. It is recommended also that houses for elderly priests should be constructed so that they may spend their old age in priestly and peaceful surroundings and with adequate care. Priests are encouraged to take care of their health, to have a regular medical check-up, and to take precautions against contagious illness, especially in places where hygienic conditions are poor.

Attitude to Wills

Among the duties concerning justice and poverty, one should not forget to draw up, in good time, a last will and testament, which should preferably be handed in to the diocesan curia. It is clear that only personal goods, not those of the Church, may be disposed of in the will. Priests should try to help the Church and the poor even after their death, and not leave their goods to those who are already well off.

CHAPTER VI

SIN OBSTACLE TO HOLINESS

Those who demand that we stay silent regarding sin are actually the ones doing humanity the greatest harm. They lull us to inactivity; imprisoning us in a condition of permanent weakness, and condemning us to a' hopeless future by calmly abandoning us to the sickness, sadness, and slavery of sin. Cancer does not grow nice by giving it new names or by not naming it at all. And neither does sin!

If those who denounce and battle against sin—personal as well as social—are lacking in compassion, then Jesus Christ must be classified as uncompassionate along with the rest. The fact is that his compassion was deeper and stronger than some can fathom. I once heard it accurately said that "Jesus loves us just as we are, but far too much to leave us that way." He loves us with all our sins, but too much to leave us in sin, far too much to keep silent about sin.

He is so compassionate that he calls us to total transformation, to a new, better, and sinless way of living. As in the case of the rich young man, his love is not just sentimental. He teaches wise and protective principles, and like any competent doctor who knows the cure, he does not hesitate to name the sickness. Its name is sin, and Jesus makes it perfectly clear that He came not for the self-righteous, who call themselves sinless, but specifically for those who suffer and are willing to confess the sickness of sin.[92] Anyone who does not talk about sin cannot be talking about the real Jesus or the revealed reason why he came. They must find new words to announce Him, deliberately avoiding the announcement made by John the Baptist: "Behold the Lamb of God who takes away the sin of the world!"[93]

Jesus came to forgive sins

Everywhere in the New Testament, we read that God gave to His son, Jesus Christ, the mission of forgiving[94] and taking away sin,[95] of giving life to sinners and leading them back to God,[96] of healing us and freeing us from

---

92   Cf. Matt. 9:12-13
93   Jn. 1:29 R.S.V.
94   Col. 1:23-24
95   Heb. 9:28
96   I Pet. 3:18

death by carrying all our sins to the cross.[97] Jesus is proclaimed as a seeker of the lost sheep,[98] an offering for our sins,[99] the one who gave His life[100] and Himself[101] for all sinners. Again and again in innumerable ways this same thing is said: He came to save sinners,[102] His name washes away our sins,[103] He redeems us by winning forgiveness for our sins.[104]

If we do not mention sin, we cannot proclaim why God became man and died such a horrible death for us on the cross. If calling sin by its name and dealing with it forcefully are signs that we lack compassion, then the teachings of Christ, His whole life, and His own passion of the cross were uniquely uncompassionate.

The Devil gives sin good names

The Devil is up to old tricks when he attempts to give sin acceptable new names.[105] But with all his ingenuity, even he has trouble making sins like these sound good: blasphemy, vengeance, gluttony, cruelty in words, lies, injustice, wrath, cruelty in actions, drunkenness, calumny, scandal, hatred, slander, arrogance, pride, bigotry, cheating, envy, promiscuity, prejudice, greed, stealing, sloth, adultery, seduction, fornication, abortion, intolerance.

We are naïve, for example, if we hear the sin called pornography gently defended as an "expression of free press" and think that the only evil involved is the possibility of some personal sexual stimulation. Even with the smallest purchase, someone is paying for the degradation and exploitation of women who are very precious daughters of God. The consumers help support an industry that is totally vile, reaching the extremes in child abuse, violent physical torture, and possibly even ritualistic murder.[106]

To this list of harmful sins of commission, we can add all the terrible sins of omission: the indifference to the poor and the needy, the neglect of the sick and the aged, the silence and inaction when witnessing oppression and injustice, and any other failure to do the good for which we were created and destined. All of these sins are acts of human selfishness, and anyone doubting the sinfulness or evil of selfishness loses his doubts once he becomes the target or victim of the selfish act.

97   I Pet. 2:24-24
98   Lk. 15:4-7
99   I. Jn. 4:10
100 I. Jn. 5:16
101 Gal. 1:3-4
102 I Tim. 1:15
103 Acts 22:16
104 Eph. 1:7
105 Gal. 5:18
106 *Newsweek*, March 18, 1985

The real names of sin are not pretty, They are the reason we call this world a "valley of tears," and the reason why Jesus was nailed to a cross. Sin just doesn't work; it never produces what it promises. Not only is it a deception; it is its very own punishment, putting us in either or both of two hells–the one here and the one hereafter. Even the shallowest of films is honest enough not to end by saying: "And they sinned happily ever after." No one ever does!

Sin may produce some quick, temporary, and apparent good. But one thing it does not produce is joy. Even less can it produce happiness, a piece of heart and a sense of personal dignity, in being who we are. This is especially true for priests! Sin in the life of a priest is a special burden and agony.

The sin we are talking about is not something ritualistically wrong simply because God arbitrarily chose to forbid it. His commandments only show that he is a loving and wise Father, and therefore must forbid evil actions that do harm to His children, while demanding the good actions essential to the right ordering of their lives. Sin weighs us down, because for a mature man it is a sin, an unchristian act of self-love, doing damage to our dignity as adopted sons of a Heavenly Father whose very nature and holiness is outpouring divine love.

Sin is Harmful

Despite all the modern propaganda to the contrary, we know deep down in our hearts that every sin is harmful, especially so when it is the sin of a priest. St. Bernard says that the sins of priests are "committed in heaven," and St. Alphonsus that they are "committed in the midst of light." This not only adds to their gravity, but also takes away any chance of claiming safe haven in the prayer of Christ, "Father, forgive them, for they know not what they are doing."

The great spiritual dignity of a priest, his role in bringing others to holiness, his place at the altar of God with Christ's word on his lips and Christ's body in his hands, all multiply the damaging effects of sin in his life. This is why we read in Leviticus[107] that the very same sacrifice of a perfect calf must be offered either for the single sin of a single priest, or for all the sins of all the people. A sinning priest brings a terrible element of scandal to the Church (lacks commitment, disobedience to the Bishop, etc.).

Sin of omission and commission

This is probably more true of sins of omission than of sins of commission. Jesus is relatively gentle with Mary Magdalene, the woman caught in adultery, and the woman with five husbands. But to the ones who do not feed the hungry, clothe the naked, take in the stranger, visit the prisoners and the sick, or refuse even a cup of water asked in his name, His words are: "Out of my sight, you condemned, into that everlasting fire prepared for the devil and his angels."[108]

About the servant who buried his talent in the ground, Christ's words are equally strong: "You worthless lazy lout!... Throw this worthless servant into the darkness outside, where he can wail and grind his teeth."[109] And when His own disciples fail to heal an epileptic boy, His obviously painful complaint is: "What an unbelievable and perverse lot you are."[110] Even when Peter's only failure is that he cannot continue walking on water, Jesus expresses a deep disappointment: "How little faith you have!... Why did you falter?"[111] And when Peter attempts to lead Jesus himself into a sin of omission by tempting him to turn back from Calvary, the criticism coming from Christ is unparalleled in its harshness: "Get behind me, Satan."[112] If sins of omission are serious for all Christians, then what about such sins in the critical mission of a priest, the most vital mission given any human being? What about simply ignoring his command that "penance for the remission of sins is to be preached to all the nations?"[113] What about his instruction that when we see our brother sinning, we should go to him and tell him his sin?[114]

What about the cruelty of leaving people disappointed, heartbroken, and in despair because their priests never talk to them about sin, never call them back from it, never proclaim that they can come back because Jesus died for them on the Cross?

And what if a priest fails in these areas not because he is convinced by the arguments that the only real sins–the only sins doing any real harm–are the "sins of society and the evils of political and social systems?" What if he were only hiding the truth with this argument and actually staying silent about the harm and victims of personal sin because he now has more sin in his own life than he wants to face or cares to admit? The Bible says that anyone who is not willing even to recognize his sins was "the clearest of

107   Lev. 4:3, 13
108   Mtt. 25:41
109   Mtt 25:26, 30
110   Lk. 9:41
111   Mtt. 14:31
112   Mk. 8:33 R.S.V.
113   Lk. 24:47
114   Mtt. 18:15

all sinners."[115] How do these words apply to the priest who no longer feels that he is able or obliged to do anything about his own personal sins, even to confess them?

Freedom from sin

Now I have said the painful things that needed to be said about sin! So I can go on to say what I am yearning to say: there is a freedom from sin! Every priest has the mission not only of being a great enemy of sin, and in this way the most authentic and Christ-like lover of sinners, but also the clearest voice proclaiming through the irrefutable witness of a saintly life, that freedom from sin is possible

We can go back to innocence! Not the make-believe, unrealistic innocence of some people, but the gloriously heroic, incomparably moving and forceful innocence of the Blessed Virgin Mary, John the Baptist, St. Francis of Assisi, and all the great hero-saints of God.

Freedom from sin by Christ

Jesus died to make freedom from sin possible. We are commanded to proclaim it and promise it to others. And so it can be done!

But it would be unfair simply to say this, without explaining just how to do it. The explanation is surprisingly clear. It is done exactly the way cripples were healed, the way the blind won back their sight, the deaf again began to hear, lepers were cleansed, and even the dead came back to life. It is done by believing in Jesus Christ and setting Him free to accomplish His mission in our lives.

Freedom from sin comes to us just the way it came to someone like the sinful woman who bathed the feet of Jesus with her tears, wiped them with her hair and anointed them in the house of Simon the Pharisee. . As Jesus Himself explained: "Your sins are forgiven."[116] It comes by believing that Jesus can, that He wants to, and that He does, set us free. "Everyone who lives in sin is the slave of sin. If the Son of man frees you, you will really be free."[117]

There is no other way: not by heroic acts of self will; not by special training programs; not by Yoga or Zen or self-help psychologies; not by reading the latest book on breaking bad habits; and not by someone else simply saying words to cast out all our evil spirits.

---

115   Cf. also I Jn. 1:8; Prov. 28:13
116   Lk. 7:48, 50
117   Jn. 8:34, 36

No! You yourself must be convinced with unshakable faith that Jesus makes this freedom available to you. No matter how powerful a certain habit, no matter what your past history of sin, no matter how great your sense of personal weakness, no matter even if you commit a certain sin again right after hearing these words, you must believe that "the One within you is greater than anything in the world."[118] Who, then, is conqueror of the world? The one who believes that Jesus is the Son of God.[119]

If we listen only to psychiatry, we will believe that the weakness of human nature is the deciding factor in why we go on doing things we know we should not do. The real reason is a failure to ask with St. Paul, "What a wretched man I am! Who can free me?" while also crying out with Paul the answer: Jesus Christ our Lord!"[120] We go on committing the very same number and kinds of sins when we believe more in our own weakness than we do in the strength that is ours in Jesus Christ. We find it easier to believe in the past history of our sins and failures than in supernatural grace and the divine power of Christ's Holy Spirit working within us. Knowing that sin is stronger than we are, we do not join ourselves through faith to the full victory of Jesus Christ, who overcame sin's greater victory, death itself. And so we go on sinning!

When St. Peter describes the Devil as "prowling like a roaring lion, looking for someone to devour," he next says, "Resist him solid in faith."[121] We begin to experience our own victory over sin when we begin to accept as literally true statements such as these, found everywhere in the New Testament: "At this they said to him, what must we do to perform the works of God? Jesus replied: This is the work of God: have faith in the one whom he sent."[122] "In his own body he brought your sins to the Cross, so that all of us, dead to sin, could live in accordance with God's will."[123] "You yourself were once alienated from him; you nourished hostility in your hearts because of your evil deeds. But now Christ has achieved reconciliation for you in his mortal body by dying, so as to present you to God holy, free of reproach and blame. But you must hold fast to faith, be firmly grounded and steadfast in it, unshaken in the hope promised you by the gospel you have heard."[124]

Each of these scriptures tells us that only Jesus can and does free us from sin. We certainly do not free ourselves! And we start to possess this freedom

---

118   I Jn. 4:4
119   I Jn. 5:5
120   Rom. 7:24-25
121   I Pet. 5:8-9
122   Jn. 6:28-29
123   I Pet. 2:24
124   Col. 1:21-23

only after we believe so fearlessly and so absolutely in Christ, that we in turn set Him totally free within us to accomplish His work of salvation.

We have not done this yet, if we are still afraid the cost may be too much, or that Jesus may take something from us that we truly need, or that the action He takes may be too painful, too sudden, too complete, or too humiliating. All of these fears are doubts, and doubts contradict our faith. They mean that we are holding back, and in this way standing in opposition to His power that saves.

If Jesus suffered unimaginable agony, shed the last drop of his blood, and gave up his life to free us of sin, He will certainly free us if only we let Him. But letting Him free us means telling Him—with absolutely no conditions or limitations—to do whatever is needed no matter what the cost, no matter what the pain, no matter what needs to be sold or given away in order to possess a sinless heart, the pearl of great price.

Allowing Him to do this also means listening to Him carefully, studying His words, and recognizing his voice, talking to Him regularly in prayer, following and obeying Him as Lord and Master, never going where He could not follow, never doing what He would not share, and following the inspiration of His Holy Spirit in all situations. Believing in Him, trusting Him, depending upon Him to this extent, and not the tiniest degree less, is the one sure road to freedom from sin. The road is there, and it is ready to be traveled.

This is the faith that sanctifies and justifies, as St. Paul teaches in his key letter to the Romans. It is not a faith without good works, but rather a faith so real and strong that it impels us to do good works and never allows us to do wrong. It is a faith that first leads us to Christ, and then always and only to wherever He takes us, following Him so closely in our lives of faith.

Our transformation will not be instantaneous. Every sin will not disappear on the spot. We can get instant coffee, tea, and almost anything else, but there is no such thing as instant sanctity. We have to stay confident in our faith through every trial and possibly through new failures and shortcomings, while moving constantly, but not always noticeably forward toward the most glorious, satisfying, and real freedom we can experience. It is the freedom to do only what is good, and to avoid everything that is evil, and we call it freedom from sin. "Sin will no longer have power over you; you are now under grace.[125]

Concupiscence, though, always remains just around the corner, making it necessary to see our freedom as always precarious. Like a delicate and precious vase, it must be appreciated and carefully protected. If we again start thinking the old thought that, Well, maybe there is some truth in what sin promises, maybe I really do need it, or if we ever doubt even for a moment that Jesus is all we need–our Way, our Truth, and our Life–then we are headed back for trouble.

The best way to protect this precious and precarious freedom is by crying out with every new victory and at the end of each day spent doing good and untouched by evil. "God has done great things in me. Holy, holy, holy is His name!"[126] By giving all the glory to God, Mary celebrated and protected her own innocence. It is the only way we can protect ours.

If we hope and believe in this way, if we set Jesus free within us, if we give God all the glory through our thanks, then we will be holy and truly free. And it will all be the work not of ourselves, but of the spotless lamb of God who has taken away our sins.

---

125   Rom. 6:14
126   Lk. 1:49

CHAPTER VII

PRAYER AND CELEBRATION OF THE EUCHARIST: KEY TO PRIESTLY HOLINESS

Living a life of prayer is not an option for a priest. He is a man of prayer. Put differently, as a man consecrated to serve the mission of the Church, a priest should be a man of prayer more than anything else. As a matter of fact, a priest without a prayer life is like a living body without blood; it is bound to die. Apart from personal prayers, reflections, and meditations, there are a set of prayers a priest has to say each day from his breviary, known as the Office of the Hours. The Church is in prayer whenever a priest says those prayers. That is why they are called liturgical prayers. The Office of the Hours unites the priest with Christ and the universal Church.

Prayer as a means to holiness has no substitute and no equal. Jesus, truly a man of prayer, lived in constant and intimate contact with his heavenly Father. And by word and example he taught that we must do the same, until we too can say that we pray always.[125]

Prayer as a means to holiness has no substitute and no equal. Jesus, truly a man of prayer, lived in constant and intimate contact with his heavenly Father. By word and example He taught that we must do the same, until we too can say that we pray always.[127]

Prayer and holiness are parallel to the degree that one cannot exist without the other. Prayer is an intimate union with the mind and heart of God, leading us to become "one spirit with Him."[128] It is a way of being in direct contact with God the Father, God the Son, and God the Holy Spirit. How could such a communion with God Himself possibly fail to sanctify?

So inseparable are prayer and holiness that if a priest finds himself losing a taste for prayer all he can do is to start praying all over again as fast as he can. When I sit in the sun, I burn. When I jump in the water, I get wet. When

---

127   Luke 18:1; 3:21; 5:16, Matt. 3:13-17; Mk. 1:9-11, Jn. 1:32-34 etc.
128   Cf. I Cor. 6 :17

I sit down in the ice, I start to freeze. In just the same way, I burn with love, feel inundated with peace, sense the cooling of selfish appetites whenever I unite myself with the holiness of God through prayer.

The Eucharist is known to be the highest prayer that the priest says. The Sacrosanctum Concilium of the Second Vatican Council teaches us that the Eucharist is the source and summit of the spiritual life. In this way the Councilor Fathers recognize the Eucharist as the center of the Church's devotional life. From the Eucharist as from a fountain, grace is channeled unto us and the sanctification and the worship of God to which all other actions of the Church are absorbed as toward their goal, are strongly accomplished(SC 39).

Whenever the Eucharist is celebrated, Christ is present in his minister, the priest. Yet the priest is fully aware that he cannot count on his own efforts to achieve the purposes of his ministry. Rather, he is called to serve as an instrument of the victorious action of Christ whose sacrifice, made present on the altar, obtains for humanity an abundance of divine gifts. However, he the priest is fully aware that he has to be profoundly connected to Christ, in order to worthily pronounce the words of consecration in the name of Christ; "This is my Body.... This is the chalice of my Blood." Note that the priest doesn't say this is the body of Christ or this is the blood of Christ. Rather he acts in the person of Christ and represents Christ there and then. He seeks to reproduce Christ's countenance in himself. The more passionately he lives in Christ, the more authentically he can celebrate the Eucharist.

> *Prayer and holiness are paralleled to the degree that one cannot exist without the other. Prayer is an intimate union with the mind and heart of God, leading us to become "one spirit with him"*

The Second Vatican Council recalled: "Priests act especially in the person of Christ as ministers of holy things, especially in the Sacrifice of the Mass" (PO 13) and that without a priest there can be no Eucharistic sacrifice. One can say here that since the priest acts in the person of Christ, (in persona Christi) as another Christ (an alter-Christos), then the priest reflects Christ to the entire Church each time he celebrates any sacrament, especially the Holy Eucharist.

However, it emphasized that those who celebrate this sacrifice must fulfill their role in intimate spiritual union with Christ, with great humility, as His ministers in the service of the community.

No wonder the Synod of Bishops recognizes the Eucharist as "the heart of the priestly existence." This means that the presbyter, desiring to be and remain personally and profoundly attached to Christ, finds Him first in the Eucharist; the sacrament which brings about this intimate union, open to a growth which can reach the heights of mystical identification.

One cannot overemphasize the fact that there is a strong connection between the priest and the Eucharist. Over the years many exemplary and wise men of God have written and made statements in affirmation of the interconnection between the priest and the Eucharist. A few examples may be of help here.

Pope John Paul II, In his General Audience of June 9th 1993, asserts that the Eucharist is at the heart of the Priest's spirituality. That same Pope in his personal letter to priests on Holy Thursday 2004 stated, "The ministerial priesthood is born, lives and works and bears fruits 'de Eucharistia." This means that in essence the priesthood was born of the Eucharist. Cardinal Avery Dulles, SJ, in his article titled, "Priest and Eucharist: No Higher Calling," enunciated that priesthood and Eucharist are profoundly interconnected. The Cardinal goes on to say that "the priest is a mediator; he offers sacrifices to God on behalf of himself and the people, and in return he distributes to the people the gifts that come from God."[129] On his part, Msgr. Stephen J. Rossetti, the author of The Joy of Priesthood, noted, "In the sacrifice of the Mass, Jesus is present in the entire assembly, but most especially in the priest."[130]

Since the priestly identity is linked directly to the Eucharist, many priests didn't experience difficulties embracing the revised translation of the Mass that was promulgated in the United States on November 27th 2011. Priests are very grateful to the Church for the new translation which better evokes

---

129 A. DULLES, "Priest and Eucharist: No Higher Calling," in S. J. ROSSETTI, (ed) *Born of the Eucharist: A Spirituality for Priests*, Ave Maria Press, Notre Dame 2009, 11-25
130 S.J. ROSSETTI, "The Eucharist: A Callto Priestly Holiness," in S.J. ROSSETTI (ed) *Born of the Eucharist: A Spirituality for Priests,* 83-100.

the original text in Latin. Furthermore, this revision helps and encourages the priests to deeper prayer and more chanting of the Mass as it roots us more in the Scripture. For example, in the greeting, The New Roman Missal brings us into the Pauline language based on the last words of Saint Paul's second letter to the Corinthians (13:13 NRSV): "The grace of our Lord Jesus Christ, and the Love of God, and the communion of the Holy Spirit be with you all." This points to the bond of Unity of the people of God and our connectedness with the Divine in worship.

This is, of course, doubly true whenever you approach the Eucharist with faith and true humility.[131] The Eucharist incorporates two unparalleled moments of Christ-centered sanctification and transformation: the consecration of the bread and wine, and the reception of Holy Communion.

During the first of these moments, the priest becomes "a living instrument" of the Holy Spirit, elevated by him to a level nothing short of divine. This produces an unheard-of effect; the true, real, and substantial changing of the bread and wine into the body and blood of Christ Himself. At this moment Jesus, the spotless lamb, is so identified with his holy priest that He uses the priest's own lips to say, "This is my body; this is my blood."[132]

During the second of these moments, as the priest receives Holy Communion, his heart becomes the dwelling place of the risen and glorified Christ. As Christ becomes the guest of our hearts, the Holy Spirit becomes his gift par excellence to us. Jesus is baptizing, anointing, sanctifying, consecrating, and surrounding us with the light of that spirit of which He is such a bottomless font. And the Spirit, in turn, is flooding our hearts with love for the Father, while transforming us into recognizable images of Jesus, the Son.

This is why a meaningful and loving celebration of the Eucharist is the pinnacle of our configuration with Christ. "All of us, gazing on the Lord's glory with unveiled faces, are being transformed from glory to glory into the very image of the Lord who is the Spirit."[133] As he celebrates the Eucharist, every priest should be crying out: Dearest Jesus, with the fire of your Holy Spirit burns your image into me, so that I might totally reflect only you!

God the Father seeks only authentic worshippers, those who will "worship him in spirit and truth."[134] In other words, he is looking for those

---

131   Cf. Jn. 6 :37-40, 56-57
132   Decree on the Ministry and Life of Priests *(Presbyterium Ordinis)* Var. 11, 1965 No. 28 p. 901
133   2 Cor. 3:18
134   Jn. 2:24

who will glorify him by following the guidance of the Holy Spirit as they live and work in union with Christ, the transforming truth.[135] This is just another way of saying that we glorify the Father only through our holiness, a holiness that comes from Jesus and His Holy Spirit, and finds its first expressions in the sanctification of others: "I have given you glory on earth by finishing the work you gave me to do."[136]

So, undaunted by fatigue or past transgressions, and with our eyes set on the awesome panorama of sanctity to which we are called, let us set out once again to reach the heights of priestly holiness. Like Peter, let us have the fullest confidence in what can happen if, at Jesus' word, we cast forth our nets.[137] As followers of God, we can move forward with St. Paul's battle cry to holiness ringing in our ears: "Brothers, I do not think of myself as having reached the finish line, I give no thought to what lies behind, but push on to what is ahead. My entire attention is on the finish line, as I run toward the prize to which God calls me–life on high in Christ Jesus.[139]

It makes no difference whether we have been ordained for only a year, or for ten or twenty-five, or even if we are celebrating our golden jubilee. For each of us, now is the right moment to humbly and confidently renew our commitment to holiness. Now is the right time to tell Jesus to work His greatest miracle by changing us into "holy ones of God," living witness of the limitless power of the Holy Spirit. All we have to do is say, "Lord, you know everything; you know well that I love you,"[140] and then simply believe that "things that are impossible for men are possible for God."[141]

God's infinite love for his priests easily outstrips the sum of all our sins and shortcomings. If it only takes a few minutes to bring out the purity of gold in the heat of a furnace, how much easier is it to refine the pure gold of our priestly holiness in the fire of the creature, priests renewed and made holy in every part of their being and in all their actions? This flame of holiness must touch the heart of every priest, so that it can be carried by them to the hearts of others!

"Sursum corda." Lift up your hearts; march forward fearlessly to holiness! This is possible because the means to holiness are in our hands. We have Jesus, the Holy one of God telling us, "The man who feeds on my flesh and drinks my blood remains in me, and I in him."[142] We have

---

135	Cf. Jn. 14:6	141	Lk. 18:27
136	Jn. 17:4	142	Jn. 6:56
137	Cf. Lk. 5:5		
138	Cf. 2 Pet. 3:8		
139	Phil. 3:13-14		
140	Jn. 21:17		

the fountain of holiness, the Holy Spirit, consecrating us and washing us clean.[143] We have the Heavenly Father, source of all holiness, as guest of our hearts just as Jesus promises: If a man loves me, my Father will love him, and we will come to him and make our home with him."[144]

St. Paul calls down on us this incomparable blessing of holiness with the prayer: "May the Father strengthen you inwardly through the working of His Spirit. May Christ dwell in your hearts by faith, and may charity be the root and foundation of your life. Thus you will be able to grasp fully, with all the holy ones, the breadth and length and depth of Christ's love . . . so that you may attain to the fullness of God Himself."[145]

To this we have the added blessing and help of Mary, the "Theotokos"(Mother of God), the mother of Christ the Priest. She who helped formed the priestly heart of Christ always prays with maternal love for all priests, so that they too can be faithful and docile to the Holy Spirit as he shapes them into that image of Christ so badly needed in the world today. Through an outpouring of the Holy Spirit, and with our own prayers united to those of Mary, may every priest on earth be a sacrificial host made pure, holy, and immaculate, a living image of Christ as both Priest and victim. And may all this be done for the praise and glory of God the Father! Amen![146]

---

143   Cf. I Cor. 6:11
144   Jn. 14:23, R.S.V.
145   Eph. 3:16-19
146   Vat. II, dogmatic Constitution *Lumen Gentium*, 1964, No. 14.

CHAPTER VIII

THE POWER OF THE CROSS

In our lives, the cross takes on a surprising variety of styles and shapes. As pointed out by our Blessed Pope John Paul II in Canada, 1984 "The shadow of the Cross permeates our priestly lives; it can take the form of illness and old age, of loneliness and discouragement, of interior trials such as the dark night of the soul, or any other torment of the heart."

We must be daily alert to the fact that because we share Christ's priesthood, our ministry bears the seal of His cross. At different times of life, the wood of that cross can be colored a thousand different hues: first with the bitter tears that come from rejection by the same society that once rejected the unborn Babe of Bethlehem; then with the heavy sweat of hard work mirroring Christ's labors in the carpenter shed of Nazareth, and finally with the deep red blood of total sacrifice, linked to the blood of Christ flowing down from Calvary.

During the International Eucharistic Congress held at Lourdes in 1981, the above mentioned Pope taught far better by example than anyone could possibly do with words. At the great event his pastoral cross was in our midst, but he himself lay seriously wounded in a hospital bed in Rome, fighting for his life after the assassination attempt that almost took him from us. This was his witness to the truth that the "breaking of the bread," so integral to every Mass, must sooner or later become a reality in our own lives, as we do our priestly part to bring to completion our salvation in Christ Crucified.[147] One nice thing that happened was that the Pope forgave his assisin.

They shall look upon Him whom they have pierced!"[148] When we contemplate Christ on the cross, and even more so when we see how He looks down from the cross at us, we have the best reason for taking joy from a "hope that will not leave us disappointed."[149] I see reflected in you as you look at Him, and in His eyes looking down with love at you, thousands of priests today are still being persecuted, tortured, killed and exiled for proclaiming faith in Christ, and for demanding justice and dignity for all. The great suffering of some is that

---

147   Cf. Col. 1:24
148   Jn. 19:37
149   Rom. 5:5

they are unable, cut off as they are from any opportunity, to proclaim the Good News, or celebrate in any public way the mysteries of redemption.

In today's environment, some priests suffer meeting only incomprehension, anger and controversy when they proclaim and faithfully live the message of Christ, even within their own communities. Others work tirelessly without seeing any fruit from their sacrifices and pastoral efforts. But more than anything else, I am thinking right now of those who suffer the agony of their own weaknesses and vulnerability. Some stay faithful, while others find themselves too battered and desperate to persevere in the fulfillment of their priestly commitments.

This fragility of human nature is actually the beginning point for grasping the mystery of the cross. Christ crucified shares and touches the depths of human frailty, making weakness itself a cause for hope. He tells us, as he told St. Paul, "My grace is enough for you, for in weakness power reaches perfection."[150]

The cross expresses the universality of Christ's redemptive love. From His elevated place of the cross, Christ's eyes sweep across the ages incorporating every generation, while His outstretched arms embrace us all. As Origen wrote, "Where man is concerned, God suffers a passion born of love."

The only adequate way to respond to such signs of love is to show that we too are willing to suffer for the good of others.

The challenge to respond with this kind of generosity is especially compelling for priests.

The first joy of the cross is the discovery of this radical love of God for all humanity; and eternal love reaching its supreme culmination at Calvary. It is a love that could not remain indifferent or powerless in the face of human need and suffering. The cross, God's self-obligation and abandonment to the cause of our salvation, seals His eternal "Yes" to humanity's cry for help. Can anything give more joy than witnessing to the faithful and innocent love of Christ, who accepted self-immolation to win for us the fullness of life? A God who has suffered for us tells us, "Come to me, all you who are weary and find life burdensome, I will refresh you... your souls will find rest, for my yoke is easy and my burden light."[151]

---

150   2 Cor. 12:9
151   Mttt. 11:28-30

Raised above us, the cross also brings joy because it proclaims that the deceptions of sin have already been conquered. Good does triumph over evil, justice over injustice, peace over war, love over hatred and life over death. Though certain manifestations of evil still remain, the final victory is won.[152] The trials and pains of life only prepare us for an eternal glory beyond our dreams, since nothing can separate us from the love of God that "has made us more than conquerors" in Jesus Crucified, "handed over for the sake of all."[153] The cross is the joy of self sacrifice, the joy of being able to give for the good of others, a willingness to do good even if it means suffering at the hand of others. It is an obligation of love that includes the giving up of time, of legitimate rights of preferred relationships, of health and even life itself in an effort to serve the needs of others. Through the mystery of the cross, the individual is liberated from dominating self-interests to the point that acts of self-giving become his source of peace and joy. As a matter of fact, once touched and liberated by the cross of Christ, self-giving becomes our best reason for lasting joy. It is the joy of loving in a way that creates love in the love-starved hearts of others.

In union with the crucified Son of God, even the most terrible suffering, loss of life itself not excepted, becomes a joy nothing less than sublime. Christ's teaching on the road to Emmaus, "Did not the Messiah have to undergo all this so as to enter into his glory?"[154] translates for us into hope and joy and a promise of glory for ourselves.

The cross truly is a sign of contradiction.[155] In today's world of devouring egotism, it is harder than ever to find anyone willing to lose his own life to save the lives of others. Where does the strength come from for doing battle with the old man, and for crucifying the urges of the flesh in order to be led by spiritual and moral demands of a far higher order?

This applies to the problem of priestly and religious vocations in the Church today. By itself new faith in family life is not enough to turn around the trend of declining vocations. A spirit of sacrifice and self-offering, the very thing so absent in modern hearts and homes, is also an absolute must.

---

152 Cf. 2 Cor. 4:17
153 Cf. Rom. 8:33-39
154 Lk. 24:26
155 Cf. Cor. 1:23

So many of today's youth rich in creature comforts, only grow melancholy like the rich young man of the Gospel,[156] when they hear the call of Christ. Focusing on the riches they already seem to have, they miss the chance to experience the greater joy offered to those who carry the cross in the footsteps of our Lord. "Eye has not seen, ear has not heard, nor has it so much as dawned on man what God has prepared for those who love him."[157]

We have traveled too far from the times and spirit of the first Christians who were "full of joy that they had been judged worthy of ill-treatment for the sake of the Name,"[158] or of St. Paul who wrote to the Colossians, "Even now I find my joy in the suffering I endure for you."[159] We are forgetting today that love becomes creative and contains redemptive power when authentic disciples share the burden of their Master's cross.[160]

"There is no greater love then this; to lay down one's life for one's friends."[161] This has been the consistent teaching of the Apostles and their successors, and the heroic witness of saintly deacons, priests and religious throughout the centuries. St. Francis of Assisi comes to mind immediately as the example 'par excellence' of saintly joy in giving all through a life of poverty and humility. Other examples would be: the Curé of Ars who signed his name with the simple words, "John Vianney, a poor priest;" Peter Claver, slave of the slaves brought from Africa; Don Bosco who learned from his mother never to forget his humble origins while working to help others, especially the young. Closer to our own times is the example of Saint Maximilian Kolbe who gave his own life to save the life of a fellow prisoner who was needed by a wife and children.

The kind of world we live in today, with its heart and soul stifled by selfish consumerism, modernity, and relativism, challenges priests in a special way to exercise the ministry of the cross. If we are needed for anything, it is to proclaim from one end of the earth to the other that no man, no woman and no nation can reach joy or realize fulfillment without passing through the pains of rebirth, without putting to death the spirit of selfishness that degrades human nature and washes away our real dignity. Joy of life is found inside the human heart, and it is reached only at the end of a path that is long, hard, and liberating. Nothing profoundly human comes effortlessly. It is the fruit of energetic struggles united to Christ's

---

56   Cf. Lk. 18:23
157   I Cor. 2:19
158   Act 5:4
159   Act 1:24
160   Cf. Mk. 8:34
161   Jn. 15:13

victory over the destructive forces of human weakness attacking us from inside out.

Vast crowds of humanity need from us not the illusions of worldly wisdom or the echoing of silly and shallow ideological trends bubbling forth from a hopeless and crisis-ridden society, but the strong, clear language of the cross. It alone contains the "power of God" for man's redemption for those chosen by Christ to bear abundant and lasting fruit.[162] Christ made known to the Apostles and all inheriting the priesthood from them, their vocation and ministry. They must be His friends, friends too of the mysteries He came to accomplish. The priesthood calls us to a special bond of friendship with the mystery of redemption through which Christ gives his flesh for the life of the world."[163] The priest or missionary who understands and lives this as His guiding light to holiness is a happy man! "The Cross, the Host, the Virgin, they are everything needed for success in the spiritual life."

To help us persevere in the quest for holiness, some of the wisest words of encouragement often come from the laity, or some members of our family. This was the case with one young priest, whose mother said to him on the day of ordination: "Son, to become a priest means to begin to suffer." She was telling him that he had to make his proclamation of Christ Crucified credible by joyfully taking up the cross himself. The message was well understood, since that young priest went on to become St. Pius X.

It is true that "neither he who plants nor he who waters is of any special account, only God who gives the growth."[164] But the sufferings of the sower, the pains of the one who waters and cultivates, still play an integral part in bringing about the ultimate joy of the reaper. God gives us the privilege and joy of experiencing the mysterious solidarity between our own weak painful efforts and the tall-powerful cross of Christ. St. Theresa of the Child Jesus, called the "most joyful of all saints," experienced this to the depths of her heart in her hidden Carmel of Lisieux. And because she understood so well the link between human weakness, the cross, and successful ministry, little Theresa declared that she wanted to spend her paradise praying for the Church and for priests.

162　Cf. Icor. 1:18
163　Doc. Cath. April, 1983
164　I Cor. 3:7

May these prayers of hers, united to those of Mary, the compassionate Virgin and heavenly Mother of all priests, win for us the joy of being authentic disciples of Christ Crucified. To be His disciples and friends means walking with Him day by day the path of the Beatitudes until finally laid to rest. We should hear Him calling us to endless joy with the words: "Come. You have my Father's blessing! Inherit the kingdom prepared for you from the creation of the world.[165]

Dear brothers and sisters, "rejoice that your names are inscribed in heaven!"[166]

---

165   Mtt. 25:35
166   Lk. 10:20

CHAPTER IX

HEALING THE WOUNDS OF LIFE

As brother priests, our own greatest need is to be filled like both Peter and Paul with the power of the Holy Spirit. It is the only way we too can be witnesses of Christ, "yes, even to the ends of the earth."[167]

In the Apostolic Exhortation, *"Evangelii Nuntiandi,"* Pope Paul VI wrote that "we live in the Church at a privileged moment of the Spirit."[168] Now the Holy Spirit leads us to a very special meeting with Jesus Christ, Lord of our lives. Adapting the vibrant words of Pope John Paul II on his visit to the Dominican Republic, we should be expecting a "personal encounter with the Risen One, our eyes open and our hearts tuned to his heart-beat."

This theme, "Healing the Wounds of Life," was chosen because there are so many wounds, either inherited or inflicted, hampering our ability to live as Christians and grow in holiness, such wounds often lead to actions and attitudes that distort the special witness to holiness expected of us as priests. Happily, the same Jesus who breaks our chains of sin and death also heals us of these wounds, so that we can realize our mission of being good and unselfishly doing good for others.

Years of work in the area of spiritual renewal have made me a close and personal observer of the inner healings Jesus is bringing about in so many wounded hearts.[169] Jesus Christ continues to heal the wounds of the wounded hearts of all who believe. "Jesus Christ is the same yesterday, today and forever."[170] Our priestly ministry will remain weak and seriously hampered, if we hold to the false idea that the caring heart of Christ is limited in its concerns only to certain areas of our being. This idea robs us of the full strength of the Holy Spirit, putting limits on his ability to fashion us into convincing witnesses of our Risen Lord.

The effectiveness of our ministry, as shepherds of God's people, depends upon the witness we give through personal holiness. It is to holiness that we must lead the flock, and the first rule for doing so never varies: "Whoever remains in me and I in him will bear much fruit, because without me, you

---

167   Acts. 1:8
168   Pope Paul VI. *Evangelii Nuntiandi* No. 75
169   Acts 4:12, Col. 1:11-13
170   Heb. 13:8

can do nothing."[171] If we believe this and are trying hard but still experience daily discouragements and sluggishness in spiritual growth, this is an indication that we are in need of deep inner healing.

Grave interior wounds can be preventing our growth in holiness first of all by flooding us with resentments. Resentments keep us from experiencing the compassionate love of Christ and from channeling that love to others who need it so desperately. A process of inner healing enables the priest to discern and communicate this love by freeing him of any lifetime accumulation of bad memories and purging him of all venomous hate. Such a healing is needed before love, the essence of holiness, can blossom in him as the first gift and fruit of the Holy Spirit.

In the book, *He Touched Me*, Fr. John Powell, S.J., gives a beautiful witness of how a personal encounter with Jesus Christ helped him to reach an exciting level of freedom and healing and a new sense of personal union with God:

> In the days that followed, I began to pray with a new intensity. From the early morning shower till the darkened moments while waiting for sleep, I kept inviting Jesus into my house of many rooms. I kept reassuring Him that I was ready to admit my own bankruptcy, my own helplessness to direct my life, to find peace and joy. I constantly invited the Holy Spirit to take down my walls, to destroy the barricades that were so many years in the building. I asked the Spirit to free me from the ingrained habit of competition, from the insatiable hunger for success, from the need for incense and adoration. What began to happen in me almost immediately can be compared only to springtime. It seemed as though I had been through a long, hard-frozen wintertime. My heart and soul had suffered all the barrenness, the nakedness of nature in winter. Now in this springtime of the Spirit, it seemed as though the veins of my soul were thawing, as though blood was beginning to course through my soul again. New foliage and new beauty began to appear in me and around me.[172]

---

171   Jn. 15:5
172   John Powell; *He Touched Me*, Dublin, 1978, p. 16

Once again I had the sensation of putting on a new pair of badly needed glasses and seeing all kinds of things that had been obscured. Without an active faith, the world can seem very alien, threatening. Human life can seem like a contest of endurance, the survival of the fittest. In the vision of faith, the world becomes warm and friendly. Other people are not really menacing. They are, in fact, my brothers and sisters, because God is our Father and Jesus is our Brother.[173]

If we open up, Jesus as Savior and Emancipator will undoubtedly be leading us too from the barrenness of winter to the needed healing of a spiritual springtime.

Only the bloom of such a spring lets us relish the richness of His love, while surrendering fearlessly to the sanctifying actions of His Holy Spirit. By healing our resentments, fears, and complexes, He makes it possible for us to focus on holiness as the ultimate goal of living, and the first requisite for successful priestly ministry.

Jesus began His own ministry by entering the synagogue of Nazareth and reading from the Book of Isaiah: "The Spirit of the Lord is upon me, because the Lord has anointed me; He has sent me to bring glad tiding to the lowly, to heal the broken hearted, to proclaim liberty to the captives, and release to prisoners, to announce a year of favor from the Lord, to place on those who mourn, a diadem instead of ashes, to give them oil of gladness in place of mourning, a glorious mantle instead of a listless spirit."[174] He made this the classic announcement of his coming to heal us in both body and soul by adding the words, "Today this Scripture passage is fulfilled in your hearing.[175]

Our Lord was given the name, Jesus ("Yahweh is salvation!"). John the Baptist announced Him as the "Lamb of God who takes away the sin of the world,"[176] not only to show Christ's determination to free us from sin, but also His readiness to deal with all the effects of sin that damage or dominate us in any way. As a Good Samaritan, Jesus comes with compassion for all who have been plundered or wounded by sin. He is ready to do whatever needs doing at any expense to Himself in order to restore our whole person to health. Pope John Paul II, in his "Apostolic Letter on Human suffering", *Salvifici Doloris*, gives us a beautiful description of this redeeming and all-embracing love of Christ.

---

173   Cf. John Powell p. 16
174   Is. 61:1-3
175   Lk. 4:21
176   Jn. 1:29

In his messianic activity in the midst of Israel, Christ drew increasingly closer to the world of human suffering. He went about doing good,[177] and his actions concerned primarily those who were suffering and seeking help. He healed the sick, consoled the afflicted, fed the hungry, freed people from deafness, from blindness, from leprosy, from the devil and from various physical disabilities, three times He restored the dead to life.[178] He was sensitive to every human suffering, whether of the body or the soul.[179]

Jesus knows that the hatreds and resentments, the fears and insecurities, the complexes of guilt and inferiority are all major obstacles standing in the way of our surrender to the Spirit's work of making us saints. Any of these, and especially any combination of them, close us off from God's plan to make us "holy and blameless in his sight."[180] Great blessings come to our ministry and our lives when the Holy Spirit guides us to the meaning of so many texts, especially in the Gospel of St. John, that describe Jesus as healer of the inner riches of our hearts.

For the healing of hatreds and resentments, we have the story of how a saving dialogue with Jesus healed a Samaritan woman so completely of her racial hatred and relational problems that she left her water jar at Christ's feet and went running through the town shouting: "Come and see someone who told me everything I ever did." Her healing, in turn, led to that of others. "Many Samaritans from that town believed in Him on the strength of the woman's word."[181] Like her, priests could do something about all the hate in the world if they themselves were transformed and healed by a personal encounter with the love of Christ. They could be leading others to a similarly salvific and healing dialogue with the Master of Love.

In our quest for holiness, we must seek Jesus as the only one able to rid us of the old wounds of hatred and resentment. Knowing that love is the only possible remedy, He commands us to love even our enemies.[182] He makes love the norm for identifying His disciples, and gives as His new commandment that all must "love one another as I have loved you."[183]

---

177   Acts 10:38
178   Is. 53:4
179   Mtt. 8:17
180   Epoh. 1:4
181   Jn. 4:29, 39
182   Mtt. 5:44
183   Jn. 13:34, 15:12

To make it possible to keep this commandment he sends his Holy Spirit, through whom "the love of God has been poured out in our hearts."[184] As promised by the prophet Ezekiel, He exchanges hearts of stone for a heart of flesh.[185] A heart transplant like this, our vengeful hearts for the forgiving heart of Christ, is a prerequisite for our renewal and sanctification.

Jesus also dedicated a major part of His salvific ministry to freeing us from the domination of fear in all its manifestations. He did this in fulfillment of the prophetic words of Zachariah, who announced that with his coming we would be "rid of fear and delivered from the enemy."[186]

We see Jesus overcoming fear in the story of Nicodemus, who first came to Christ only under cover of night for fear of the Jews.[187] Nicodemus eventually receives such radical healing and new courage that he openly defends Jesus to the Sanhedrin[188] and accompanies Joseph of Arimathea in boldly requesting from Pilate permission to remove the body of Christ from the cross.[189]

To animate and strengthen us today, Jesus repeats exactly what He told His first disciples: "It is I, do not be afraid![190] Do not live in fear, little flock. It has pleased your Father to give you the kingdom.[191] When terrified by a storm, those same disciples cried out, "Lord save us! We are lost!" And Jesus responded, "Where is your courage? How little faith you have!"[192]

Jesus deals immediately with the fears of the Apostles when He appears to them after the Resurrection and begins by saying: "Peace to you!... Why are you disturbed?"[193] He has the same kind of concern for priests today. He wants them to have His peace. He wants them to be freed of fear, delivered from dejection and worries. He offers the love of His own priestly heart as the best solution to all groundless fear. As St. John tells us, "Love has no room for fear, rather, perfect love casts out all fears."[194] If we are with someone infinitely powerful who loves us as much as Jesus, how can we be afraid?

The Gospel also offers beautiful passages telling us how the compassionate love of Christ worked to heal the scars and wounds of human complexes and emotional insecurities. In the parable of the Prodigal Son, the father is so lavish in his love and mercy that he does not give his repentant son time to repeat his practiced words of self-debasement; "Treat me like one of your hired hands." We are told that the father "ran out to

---

184	Rom. 5:5	190	Jn. 6:2
185	Cf. Ex. 36:26	191	Lk. 12:32
186	Lk. 1:74	192	Mtt. 8:25
187	Cf. Jn. 3:2	193	Lk. 24:36, 38
188	Jn. 7:50-52	194	I Jn. 4:18
189	Jn. 19:38-39		

meet him, threw his arms around his neck, and kissed him."[195] Healed not only by forgiveness, but also by such tender manifestations of love, the son could delight in the feast of reconciliation the father prepared and celebrated with him.

We see an identical gentleness and caring demonstrated towards the humiliated woman caught in adultery. All Jesus says to her are the healing words: "Nor do I condemn you. You may go. But from now on, avoid this sin."[196]

St. John's Gospel, which can rightly be called the "Gospel of Inner Healing," ends with a description of how Jesus freed Peter from a guilt Complex, resulting from having denied his beloved Master three times. Forgiveness came to him as soon as he shed bitter tears for his sin.[197] But Jesus did even more! The depression of guilt incurred at the fireside in the high priest's courtyard is washed away at another fireside on the shore of the Sea of Tiberias. Three times Peter is given the opportunity to tell Jesus that he loves Him, even more than the others. And not once does Jesus deny it. He simply directs Peter to channel that love towards feeding Christ's sheep and little lambs. He was confirming Peter as His vicar even after the triple denial, and by this confirmation heals him of his devastating complex of guilt. This is why Peter could with full confidence proclaim to us, "Cast all your worries on Him because He cares for you."[198]

We can expect such inner healings of the past to be repeated today because this Jesus who heals is the same yesterday, today, and forever. We must be in prayer at His feet, attentive to His healing words. Then, like Mary of the Gospels, we will have the better portion and it will not be taken from us.[199] Jesus will touch our lives through a marvelous process of inner healing. His Spirit of love will change our wounded hearts making them holy; shaping us into competent channels of holiness and healing for countless others.

> Behold; I will treat and assuage the city's wounds; I will heal them and reveal to them an abundance of lasting peace. I will change the lot of Judah and the lot of Israel, and rebuild them as of old. I will cleanse them of all the guilt they incurred by

---

195   Lk. 15:19-20
196   Jn. 8:11
197   Cf. Lk. 22:62
198   I Pet. 5:7
199   Cf. Lk. 10:42

sinning against me; all their offences by which they sinned and rebelled against me I will forgive. Then Jerusalem shall be my joy, my praise, my glory, before all the nations of the earth, as they hear of all the good I will do among them.[200]

Lord, wounded we come to you today, filled with trust and confidence. Be our Samaritan, pitying us, binding our wounds, and pouring over us the wine and the oil of your healing love. Help us to seek you constantly in all our prayers, so that through a loving dialogue with you, the process of our inner healing might take effect. Help us to experience this healing most especially in the sacraments of Reconciliation and Eucharist.

You are the spring for which we thirst. Allow us to drink and never stop drinking, so that we never thirst again. Keep your promise, and raise up within us wells of living water. Give us your healing Spirit of Holiness, so that we might bring the waters of life to others.

We ask so much because, as King of Glory, your promises are vast and inexhaustible. You have already given yourself for us on the cross. So we know that now you will heal us and then use us lovingly for the healing and sanctification of others. We ask all this knowing that it has already been done. So we thank you, Lord. Amen!

---

200   Jer. 33:6-9

CHAPTER X

MOTHER MARY AND PRIESTS

Whoever enters into a specially close relationship with Christ thereby enters also upon a specially close relationship with His Mother, Mary.

The words which our dying Divine Savior spoke from the cross, "Woman, behold thy son; son, behold thy Mother"[201] were addressed to the apostle John, and by extension through him to all believers. This also applies to all priests of our Lord Jesus Christ in a special way.

The motherhood of Mary has a broader meaning in relation to priests. "How does this happen?" one may like to ask. How does Mary exercise her motherhood over the mystical Body of Christ? Well, the answer is that she does so above all through the priestly activities of priests. For she has a part, in some manner, in every conferring of grace. No wonder the Church teaches that Mary is the "Mediatrix of all graces." Vatican II tells us that she is "our Mother in the order of grace." As a priest, whenever, you baptize a child, reconcile a sinner with God, give the sacred food of Holy Communion, help the dying to insert their death into the sacrificial death of Christ and thus complete His saving passion and death, when you instruct the young and teach and guide the adults–all these you accomplish in affinity to Jesus Christ, sensing the motherhood of Mother Mary in your ministry. Ordinarily, children always feel their mothers' love at all times.

These indicate no doubt the special kind of devotion to Mary that should characterize us priests. We should be consciously aware of being in the service of Mary, of being privileged to help her realize her role of Motherhood over the mystical Body of the Lord. And thus we are and will remain most intimately united to Mary: we are sons; she is the Mother of the entire mystical Body of the Lord. Priests should pray earnestly to emulate the virtues of Mary their Mother and thanking God with Mary.

Jesus could never have made her His gift, unless she first gave herself to God. God was given the first place in her life; His will for her was supreme.[202] She surrendered to His own plans and wishes, accepting Him as the Lord

---

201 Jn. 19:26-27
202 Vat. II Dogmatic Constitution on the Church *Lumen Gentium* Vat. II, 1964 No. 58

of every moment she lived. Because Mary emptied herself, God could fill her with Himself. And that is how she became "Blessed among women,"[203] a woman who was fully herself. The words of the hymn, "lose yourself in me, and you will find yourself," became a reality for her and she longs to see these words become reality for us as well.

This total surrender was costly, and for much of her life Mary had to walk in darkness guided only by faith. Her whole life was rooted in that faith, and in her great love for God. The peacefulness of her question, "How can this be since I do not know man?" and the completeness of her surrender, "I am the handmaid of the Lord; let it be done to me as you say,"[204] are both expositions of this faith. Her silence when faced with the confusion of St. Joseph upon finding her pregnant is another eloquent testimony to her unshakable faith in the providence of God. That faith passed its most terrible test when she saw her son hanging like a criminal on the cross, seemingly cursed by God[205] and when the dead body of Jesus was placed in her lap. Her strength echoes the words of St. Paul: "I know him in whom I have believed, and I am confident."[206]

Priests and religious must always look up to Mary as a model and Mother for all Mary had to show here on earth, for her total surrender to God, for her cooperation carried out by her obedience, faith, hope, and burning charity in the divine plan for the world. In view of this, God decided that she should be the woman who would give birth to the Messiah. Thus she became the Mother of Jesus Christ. Jesus, in turn, gave His Mother to us as a gift. As Lumen Gentium puts it, "for this reason she is a mother to us in the order of grace."[207]

Not much affirmation or stroking here, but Mary never complained and never weakened. I believe we need this gift of Jesus, called Mary, as a Mother. It sounds strange for some, but it is true. Unfortunately some people are of the opinion that we do not need Mary. This group of people say that we should always go directly to Jesus Himself. They claim that Vatican II downplayed devotion to Mary by not dedicating a special document to her cult. The fact is that one of the special merits of Vatican II is its wisdom in not placing Mary above or outside the Church. Giving her a document of her own would be like some splendid isolation. Rather, Vatican

203   2 Tim. 1:12
204   Lk. 1:42
205   Lk. 1:34-38
206   Cf. Dt. 21:23
207   Vat. II, Dogmatic Constitution, *Lumen Gentium*, No. 58

II placed Mary squarely within the Church by treating her in the dogmatic Constitution on the Church as "Mother of God" in the mystery of Christ and the Church."[208]

In deciding to bring us forgiveness through the mystery of the Incarnation, God needed and chose Mary from among billions of women. If we claim that we can and should go to Jesus without Mary, we are arrogantly telling God that even though he needed Mary to bring us Jesus, we do not need her at all in order to go to Jesus!

Minical Parekh, who died in 1967 at the age of 82, belonged to a Jain family and became a Christian when a long illness led him to the reading of the Bible and the "imitation of Christ." He eventually entered the Anglican Church and wrote of Mary: "Virginity, sisterhood, wifehood, and motherhood became sanctified as they never were before, and woman ceased to be looked upon as a person to be exploited for man's pleasure or position."[209]

Religious, social, and domestic life became holier and sweeter, and new spirit pervaded the whole of life. Jesus came to be worshipped as the divine child in the lap of his mother, consecrating and sanctifying thus both motherhood and childhood. This devotion to Mary with the divine child, besides softening and beautifying the manners of people, has enriched immensely the art and literature of Europe.[210] In some respects, all of this formed in the past one of the greatest glories of Christendom when it was undivided, and does the same today for the Roman Catholic Church everywhere. Some Protestants threw this cult overboard, dubbing it a gross superstition and idolatry, and thus took away from the life of its followers some of the richest demands of religious, social, and domestic life.

We have every reason to be proud of Mary, the beautiful gift Christ gave us. If we honor our heroes and sportsmen and statesmen, all the more should we treasure and honor Mary in recognition of her exalted position both in heaven and on earth. We should continue to speak about her in a way that shows the whole world that we are proud to be her children. No human being redeemed by Christ will ever match the degree of holiness that is hers. She became "full of grace" not only because God showered His grace upon her, but also because to that grace she was always so completely open and totally receptive.

---

208   Ibid
209   Minical C. Parekh, Bkl, p. 103
210   John Paul II *Pastores Dabo Vobis* 1992, p. 63

If some object that we honor her too much, my answer is that they must direct their objections to God the Father. After all, it was He who made her mother of God. And all of us together could never have given her a more exalted title. So God Himself should be the first they criticize, if anyone has given to Mary "too much honor."

Christ gives us the gift of His Blessed Mother without any strings attached. But it would be foolish to give no gift in return. As priests, the best response to Christ's gift of Mary is to give ourselves to her as sons. She can then make us her gift to Christ, who in turn gives us to the

We can start judging our priestly success only in terms of the concrete and visible spiritual growth. We can start to torment ourselves by asking, "What do I have to show for my ten, twenty, thirty years of priesthood? Just what have I succeeded in doing or achieving?"

world. Before we can fulfill our priestly mission, we too must be led by the example and prayers of Mary to empty ourselves, so that we can be filled with the holiness of God. Then with St. Paul, we can say, "the life I live now is not my own; Christ is living in me."[211] If Paul can tell us to imitate him as he imitates Christ,[212] with how much greater reason can Mary call us to imitate the way she so closely imitated the faith and love of her divine son.

Unless we first empty of ourselves so that through His spirit, Jesus can grow within us, we will never succeed in giving Jesus to the world. We will be giving only ourselves, and that is a poor substitute despite any zealous efforts and all our talents. The world, even without knowing it, yearns to be given Christ and nothing less.

There is danger that we priests are becoming children of our technological age, rather than remaining the humble children of God and Mary.

We can start judging our priestly success only in terms of the concrete and visible spiritual growth. We can start to torment ourselves by asking,

---

211 Gal. 2:20
212 I Cor. 11:1

"What do I have to show for my ten, twenty, thirty years of priesthood? Just what have I succeeded in doing or achieving?"

Here again is where Mary our mother can set straight our priorities. She proclaims, "God who is mighty has done great things for me, holy is his name,"[213] and these words tell us that the first thing to ask is not, "What am I going to do for God and the people I serve?", but rather, "What am I going to allow God to do for me? How am I going to let Him use me for the service of His people?" It was through obedience and surrender that Mary conceived Christ and gave the world its Savior. Redemption came because she allowed God to overshadow her with His Holy Spirit. Mary was not passive, but dynamically receptive as she offered God the holiness He found so pleasing: the surrender of her own plans and desires to His will.

---

213   Lk. 1:49

CHAPTER XI

LAY PRIESTHOOD

The members of Christ's faithful share in the priesthood of our Lord Jesus Christ. I wonder how many of our lay Christians today are aware of this reality and to the degree in which they share in this?

St. Augustine writes, "We call everyone 'priests' because all are members of only one priesthood."[214] Vatican II Document, *Lumen Gentium* (A Dogmatic Constitution on the Church) ushered in a new awareness of the dignity and roles of the laity in the Catholic Church today. First Peter introduced a new aspect of the grace and dignity coming from baptism, "You are a chosen race, a royal priesthood, a holy nation, God's own people, that you may declare the wonderful deeds of him who called you out of darkness into his marvelous light."[215]

By the waters of Baptism, a layperson becomes a member of the Mystical Body of Christ the priest, and by the indelible character imprinted upon him/her. He/she is privileged to share in the priesthood of Jesus Christ. Through the sacrament of Confirmation, Christ has set upon him or her His special seal as a sign of complete dedication to His service. This sacrament marks the highest degree of participation laymen and women can reach in the hierarchical apostolate of the church. It ordains the Christian for the work of spreading and strengthening the kingdom of Christ in the world.

Lumen Gentium spells out that the lay faithful participate for their part in the threefold mission (Trimunera) of Christ as Priest, Prophet and King. Our Holy Father, Pope John Paul II in his Apostolic Exhortation, *Christi Fedeles Laici,* The vocation and mission of the lay faithful, states, "The lay faithful are invited to take up again and re-read, meditate on and assimilate with renewed understanding and love, the rich and fruitful teaching of the council which speaks of their participation in the threefold mission of Christ."[216]

The lay faithful are sharers in the priestly mission for which Jesus Christ offered Himself on the cross and continues to be offered in the celebration

---

214   Ryan D. Williams: *The Other Christ*, p. 60
215   I Pt. 2:4-5, 9
216   John Paul II Christ *Fedeles Laici* 14

of the Eucharist, for the glory of God and the salvation of humanity.[217] It is a participation given to each member of the lay faithful individually, in as much as each is one of the many who form the one body of the Lord. In fact, Jesus showers His gifts upon the Church, which is His body and His spouse in such a way that individuals are sharers in the threefold mission of Christ by virtue of their being members of the Church. All the baptized viewed as "a chosen race, a royal priesthood, a holy nation, God's own people,"[218] is Priestly, because it derives from the Church's communion, the sharing of the lay faithful in the threefold mission of Christ. This requires that it be lived and realized in communion and for the increase of communion itself. Incorporated in Jesus Christ, the baptized are united to Him and to His sacrifice in the offering they make of themselves and their daily activities.[219] Speaking of the lay faithful, the Council says: "For their work; prayers and apostolic endeavors, their ordinary married and family life, their daily labor, their mental and physical relaxation, if patiently borne–all of these become spiritual sacrifices acceptable to God through Jesus Christ[220] to be offered in the celebration of the Eucharist, for the glory of God and the salvation of humanity."

At this juncture, it is good to redress the misconception and abuses of some people's understanding of the terminology "common priesthood." This clarification becomes necessary in order to clear the doubts on the sense in which common priesthood is applied to the laity and their role in the mission of our Lord Jesus Christ as different from the ministerial priesthood. The term "common priesthood" was one of the major issues of dispute during the Protestant reformation.

Martin Luther and the reformers claimed this common priesthood on the basis of their principle of *sola scriptura*, that is, "Scriptures alone." From this, they argued that if there is any priesthood at all in the Church, it is the priesthood that the laity share in by virtue of Baptism. Thus, the Protestants believe only in the common priesthood of all the baptized.

Many of these anti-clerical tendencies today are promoted by these groups of people. The participation of the faithful in the threefold mission of Christ as priest, prophet and king finds its source in the anointing of Baptism, its further development in Confirmation and its realization and dynamic sustenance in the Holy Eucharist.[221]

---

217   Ibid No 14
218   I Pt. 29
219   Cf. Rom. 12:1-2
220   Cf. I Pt. 2:5
221   Ibid.

Lumen Gentium beautifully brings out the difference between the common priesthood of the faithful and the ministerial or hierarchical priesthood. It must be noted that the lay priesthood must not be confused with the ministerial priesthood of those consecrated and ordained for the ministry. On this note the hierarchy must be careful of the many anti-clerical tendencies today in the Church. These tendencies promote philosophies that undermine the sublimeness of the ministerial priesthood. That is why Lumen Gentium says: "To the Ministerial or Hierarchical Priesthood belongs the Power of Teaching and Ruling in the Church. Care must be taken not to minimize the excellence of the ministerial priesthood, that its participation of the priesthood of Christ, differs from the common priesthood of the faithful, not only in degree, but in essence."[222]

Care should be taken in describing the priestly ministry. Here the emphasis is that it brings out clearly the mediation between God and men which they exercise not only in preaching the Word of God, in forming the Christian Community and in administering the Sacraments, but also and chiefly in offering the Eucharistic sacrifice in the name of the whole Church.[223]

The ministerial priesthood

The ministerial priesthood by virtue of the sacred power he has, and by virtue of consecration and ordination, forms and rules the priestly people; in the person of Christ he effects the Eucharistic sacrifice and offers it to God in the name of the people.[224]

Priesthood of the Laity

The laity exercise their royal priesthood through participating in the offering of the Eucharist; by reception of the Sacraments, prayer, thanksgiving, witness of a holy life, full civil involvement, government or private, missionary activities, laity movements, association/societies and overall collaboration with their pastors in overall pastoral life of the parish.[225]

---

222   Cf. Conc. Vat. II Const. *Lumen Gentium,* n. 10, *Instructio de Cultu Mysteril eucharistici,* AAS, 59 (1967) n. 11, p. 548
223   Cf. Conc. Vat. II Const. *Lumen Gentium,* n. 28; Decr. Presbyterium ordinis, m 2, 13
224   Pastoral Guide p. 45
225   Ibid.

CHAPTER XII

A PRIEST: LOVER OF THE POOR

"The spirit of the Lord God is upon me, because the Lord has anointed me; He has sent me to bring glad tidings to the lowly, to heal the brokenhearted, to proclaim liberty to the captives and release to the prisoners . . . to comfort all who mourn."[226]

In the synagogue of Nazareth, Jesus read this passage to announce the mission the Father had given Him and to set the tone for His public ministry. As the text is quoted by St. Luke, Jesus refers to the lowly, to whom he must announce the good tidings simply as the "poor."[227]

For Jesus, the "poor" are not limited to those who have financial problems or lack certain material necessities or political freedoms. They are also the sick of every kind, the poorly educated, those vexed by the devil, or for any reason, deprived of peace of heart and mind; but most of all, the poor are those being crushed by the slavery of sin. With statements like these, Jesus showed His constant concern for every form of human poverty: "Come to me, all who are weary and find life burdensome, and I will refresh you." "If anyone thirsts, let him come to me." "I come that they might have life, and have it to the full." "I have come to call sinners!"[228]

This is why we see Him healing all the sick who are brought to Him, casting out demons, and even raising the dead. This is why we see Him feeding crowds with His words and promise, not only with loaves and fishes, and why He welcomes those shunned by others: the lepers, the tax collectors and the public sinners. This is why we see Him freeing them from their sins: the woman caught in adultery, the paralytic, the prostitute, the soldiers crucifying Him, and the repentant thief hanging at His side on another cross.

He did everything Isaiah prophesied by giving sight not only to the physically blind, but to the intellectually and spiritually blind as well. He went out of his way to heal the broken heart of Peter who denied him thrice, and was constantly freeing those imprisoned with mental and spiritual

---

226   Is. 61:1-2, Lk. 4:18-19
227   Ibid.
228   Mtt. 11:28; Jn. 7:37, 10:10, Mtt. 9:13

oppression, as well as those enslaved by sinful passions and appetites. He even comforted the mourning parents of the little dead girl, the widow of Naim, and the sisters of Lazarus by bringing these loved ones back to life.

When John the Baptist sent his disciples to ask if Jesus was "he who is to come," Jesus who at that very moment was "curing many of their diseases, affliction, and evil spirits . . . restored sight to many who were blind," simply answered, "Go and report to John what you have seen and heard. The blind recover their sight, cripples walk, lepers are cured, the deaf hear, dead men are raised to life, and the poor have the good news preached to them."[229]

All these beneficiaries of Christ's saving power are rightly called the "poor." As a matter of fact, that word embraces all mankind impoverished by sin both original and personal, and all those wounded in heart, mind, body, or soul, by sin's sad consequences. It embraces the whole human race in need of God's healing touch, and reveals God's desire that the entire world be "freed from its slavery to corruption and share in the glorious freedom of the children of God."[230]

How true those words of the Master: "The poor you will always have with you."[231] Even today, we have them in the developed as well as the developing countries; in Europe and North America as well as in Africa and Asia. We have the spiritually bankrupt as well as the physically handicapped. We have the widows and the orphans, the elderly and forgotten, in and out of comfortable homes and good hospitals. We have the confused and retarded, but also the psychologically brilliant suddenly finding themselves unloved. We have those who are oppressed and rejected by their own families and friends, as well as those suffering political and economic repression. All are simply different categories of God's "poor."

In the countries where human liberties and human rights are flagrantly violated, it is natural, and there is every right. to think of those being oppressed and persecuted as God's poor. But the oppressors and the persecutors are also poor; they are politically powerful but utterly weak spiritually. They too are God's children. They too must be helped, loved, and offered salvation. They also are included in Christ's words: "I have come to call, not the self-righteous, but sinners."[232] This is the specific character of a true Christian:

---

229   Lk. 7:20-22
230   Rom. 8:21
231   Mtt. 26:11
232   Mtt. 5:44-46

"Love your enemies, pray for your persecutors. This will prove that you are sons of your heavenly Father, for His sun rises on the bad and the good, He rains on the just and the unjust. If you love those who love you, what merit is there in that?"[233] This was His example when He prayed for those who mocked him and nailed Him to the Cross: "Father, forgive them; they do not know what they are doing."[234]

God's poor fall into a variety of categories, and it is not our job to discriminate. The world can choose which to pity and which to despise, but Christians must be interested in the good of all. On the road to Damascus, Jesus spoke gently to a persecutor of the Church called Saul, and transformed him into the Apostle and Martyr, Paul. As an 'alter Christus' every priest must follow this example. His love for the poor must be universal, seeking salvation for all and condemnation for none.[235]

Priests like Christ, are anointed and sent to bring the Good News to all the poor. But to be of service to all, they must be busy leading them to holiness, alleviating their spiritual and emotional sufferings as well as those that are physically and materially in need. Priests must practice and teach both the corporal and spiritual works of mercy. About bad shepherds Ezekiel writes, "You did not strengthen the weak, nor heal the sick, nor bind up the injured. You did not bring back the strayed, nor seek the lost... My sheep were scattered over the whole earth, with no one to look after them, or to search for them." The description the prophet then gives of God as Good Shepherd is exactly the opposite: God seeks the lost sheep, rescuing them from wherever they have been scattered, leading them to good pastures and restful waters, binding up the injured, healing the sick, while also watching over the fat and the strong and feeding all in justice.[236] It is this example as given flesh in the person of Jesus Christ that every holy priest must follow.

The *Roman Martyrology* is filled with the names of saintly priests who did just that. Some founded religious institutes for preaching, teaching, counseling, and for healing human hurts. Others established schools and hospitals, clinics and orphanages, and homes for the handicapped, aged and abandoned. Still others worked for the rights of the oppressed, the ransoming of slaves, and the return of peace and justice to families, tribes, and nations.

---

233   Mtt. 9:13
234   Lk. 23:34
235   Jn. 3:17
236   Cf. Ex. 34:4-6

They did all these things because they had the heart of Christ and therefore a love for all God's poor.

A priest today—even if his tasks are administrative or academic, whether he works in the chancery, or university, or chaplaincy, or even in the diplomatic corps of the Holy See—must also be reaching out to every category of God's poor, living not only for them but with them as well.

There must be a warm, personal, pastoral, never patronizing relationship between him and the poor around him. Good shepherds give their lives for their sheep (Cf. Jn. 10:11), and our constant availability and identity with all the poor is dying in slow motion that shows our love to be truly Christ-like.

The love of Christ impels us."[237] This should be the motto of all priests. Our love is proven genuine when in a way it becomes nothing less than Divine. It is not tied to or tied down by merely human ideologies or even theologies. It is a Shepherd's love unable to count the cost, a love going beyond the limits of hurt, a love that seeks no reward. It is the love described by St. Paul as patient and kind, never jealous or snobbish or rude, never self-seeking or prone to anger or brooding over injuries, unlimited in its forbearance and ability to trust and hope and endure.[238]

This kind of Christ-like love is humble, and free of the holier-than-thou attitudes of the Pharisees. It is compassionate like the heart of Christ when He healed all the sick brought to Him, and fed the crowds in the streets, and raised the son of the widow of Naimes and the brother of Mary and Martha, spoke of the people as a flock without a shepherd, cried over Jerusalem, and told the parables of the lost sheep and the prodigal son The love of Christ always leads to generous service. "The Son of Man has not come to be served but to serve–to give his life in ransom for the many."[239] "If I washed your feet–I who am Teacher and Lord–then you must wash each other's feet."[240]

"Though he was in the form of God . . . he emptied himself and took the form of a slave, being born in the likeness of man."[241] Christ did not lose or try to keep secret His divinity, but He did become our servant and slave by identifying with our human condition, and by carrying to the Cross all our infirmities and all our sufferings.[242] In the same way, without losing or

---

237   2 Cor. 5:14
238   1 Cor. 13:4-7
239   Mtt. 10 :45
240   Jn. 13 :14
241   Phil. 2 :6-7
242   Cf. Mt. 8 :17

hiding our special priestly identity, by appearing to be just another group of social workers, we too must concern ourselves with the needs of all God's poor. By our ordination, we are called to be Christ-like shepherds, and this means that we too must empty ourselves to the point of being servants and slaves of all. I see each bishop and priest as that privileged creature. We have that same role of lifting up Christ, so that all can see Him and sing His praises, while strewing His path with good deeds and sacrifices motivated by love. Like that donkey, we cannot be distracted by all the shouts of praise and admiration, knowing they are not for us but for the Christ we carry and lift on high. Like that donkey, our only concern must be to move forward in holiness and humility, with a docility and determination that can be useful to the Christ we carry as He leads His rejoicing people to Paradise.[243]

The first secret of seeing the poor effectively is to be poor ourselves. "For your sake he made himself poor though he was rich,, so that you might become rich by his poverty."[244] He became materially poor by being born of a poor maiden from Nazareth in a manger of Bethlehem. He suffered another kind of poverty, the poverty of persecution, when Herod sought to kill Him, and He became a refugee fleeing from Egypt. After this He led for thirty years, the modest life of a carpenter in Nazareth, living this time in poverty of filial obedience to Joseph and Mary. In His public life, He had nowhere to lay His head, and was systematically attacked and criticized by the Scribes and Pharisees, their hatred and oppression now become a manifestation of his poverty. In the Garden Gethsemane, He was betrayed, denied and abandoned by His chosen Apostles, rejection the added element in His poverty.

Afterwards, He was condemned to an unjust and miserable death, hanging on the Cross stripped of clothing, ridiculed by his enemies, shunned by those he had cured and fed. Humiliation is his poverty. And just before He breathed His last, He gave to His beloved disciple, John, and to all of us, His last and most precious possession on earth, His Mother, Mary. Then by giving up His spirit, His poverty is completed! To make us rich in supernatural life and divine grace, and share with us His Sonship as children of God, He had become new form, not a man, the son of men, despised by the people."[245] To this same "poverty of spirit" all shepherds of Christ's flock are called, so that the sheep might grow rich.

---

243   Call to Holiness p. 95

244   2 Cor. 8:9

245   Is. 22:7

Let me conclude this chapter by pointing out that among the poor we can number some of our own brother priests. Their poverty can be spiritual, cultural, physical, mental, economic, social, or political. Whatever the case, we have a special responsibility and must give them every priority in our pastoral solicitude, and our universal concern for God's poor.

As a prelude to their priestly ordination at the Last Supper, Christ washed the feet of His Apostles. The instructions He then gave are as significant for priests today as they were for Peter and the others on that momentous night: "What I just did was to give you an example: as I have done, so you must do. I give you a new commandment: love one another. Such as my love has been for you, so must your love be for each other. This is how all will know that you are my disciples: your love for one another."[246]

This is how all Christ's priests are to be recognized, by the way they share His eternal priesthood, bringing the Good News of His love to all the poor.

---

246   Jn. 13:15, 34, 35

CONCLUSION

Just because your journey of reading this book is coming to an end does not mean that we have said everything about the priesthood. As a matter of fact, our discussion on how a priest is a "Man for God and for Others" has just begun and must continue. The concept of priesthood and priests' relationship with God and humanity is inexhaustible in the area of the spiritual life.

"Don't let yourselves be shaped by the world where you live, but rather by the will of God: What is good, what pleases, what is perfect."

I believe also that Jesus' valedictory speech to His Apostles applies to the priest. Jesus made their position in the world clear from the onset. Even though the Apostles lived in the world, they were not of the world.

"But you are not of the world since I have chosen you from the world; because of this the world hates you."

It is a known biblical fact that a priest is a man, he is chosen from among men and appointed for men and women. Note that his appointment for mankind is specifically for the things that pertain to God. In other words, priests are ordained for the spiritual affairs of men and women. In imitation of Jesus, they offer gifts and sacrifices for sin.

The Lord Jesus Christ has special love for His ministers and prays for them. "I pray for those you have given me. . . that they may be one even as we are one. . . . guard them from the evil one. As you sent me into the world, so I have sent them into the world. I consecrate myself for their sake now, that they may be consecrated in truth."

A deep consciousness of this intimate relationship of priests with the person, the mission, and the holiness of Christ led St. Paul to exclaim: "This makes us ambassadors for Christ, God as it were appealing through us."

By virtue of their anointing of the Holy Spirit, priests are marked with a special character, and are so configured to Christ, the priest, so that they can act in the person of Christ the Head to build up and establish His whole Body, which is the Church's ministry of Word, sacrament, and generosity.

It is true that priests are set apart by their consecration/ordination and position in some way in the midst of the people of God. This is not in order that they should be separated from their people or from any man/woman, but that they should be completely consecrated to the task for which God chooses them.

They could not be the servants of Christ unless they were witnesses and dispensers. Priests would be powerless to serve men if they remained aloof from their life and circumstances.

By their special ministry, priests should not conform themselves to the world. Still, it requires at the same time that they should live among men and women in this world and that as good shepherds they should know their sheep and should also seek to lead back those who do not belong to this fold, so that they too may hear the voice of Christ, and there may be one fold and one shepherd.

The laity should, on their part, support priests in their arduous task of ministry. The solidarity of the laity done through prayer, love, respect, and cooperation will go a long way in enhancing the necessary virtues of the priest's holy office amongst them. A priest, in loving his parishioners, should not lose sight of the fact that one day he is going to give an account of his stewardship to his Master for every one of you. A priest is the doctor of your souls; visit him at Mass and at the confessional. The more you take advantage of the Sacrament of Reconciliation, the holier your priests become. Confession helps a priest to reflect on his own sins and to ask for God's mercy for himself and for others. The more he offers sacrificial offerings, the holier the people of God become. At the end it will be a win-win situation. So keep loving your priests in your prayers as often as you can.

Prayer for Priest

O Jesus/ our great High Priest/ hear my humble prayers on behalf of your priests./ Give them a deep faith/ a bright and firm hope/ and a burning love/ which will ever increase/ in the course of their priestly life.
In their loneliness/ comfort them/ In their sorrows/ strengthen them/

In their frustrations/ point out to them that it is through suffering/ that the soul is purified/ and show them that they are needed by the Church/ they are needed by souls/ they are needed for the work of redemption.

O Loving Mother Mary/ Mother of Priests/ take to your heart/ your sons who are close to you/ because of their priestly ordination/ and because of the power which they have received/ to carry on the work of Christ/in a world which needs them so much.

Be their comfort/ be their joy/ be their strength/ and especially help them/ to live and to defend the ideals of consecrated celibacy.

Amen

✠John Joseph Cardinal Carberry
Former Archbishop of St. Louis

Appendix I

Father Fidelis restores faith of a wayward disciple – me

I did not enter into a conversation with the Rev. Fidelis Igwenwanne to have my faith restored, but that is what happened.

"I am so lucky, so privileged, I just wish to share my sense of excitement, my passion with everyone I meet," said Father Fidelis, a Roman Catholic priest originally from Nigeria. "There is so much to be grateful for and to believe in. So many ways we can work together to make this a better place."

Among those of us who are born into a long-standing belief system and learn its tenets at an early age, conviction can sometimes drift into indifference. Or worse, we grow skeptical of the dogma and disillusioned with leadership. Converts are recast as cynics.

Father Fidelis can change that. He can reshape a doubter into a devotee, an agnostic into a believer.

I'm not sure how successful he is at transforming atheists into Christians, but if you were to spend even a little time chatting with him, you'd find yourself wanting to reinvigorate what you were lucky enough to become at birth and what Father Fidelis has just become–an American citizen.

"I must say, it is still like a dream for me," said Father Fidelis. (It's what everyone calls him. Much easier than trying to pronounce his last name.) "It is like what I see when a person converts to Christianity. They are so passionate about their faith. It is not something that they take for granted. They made a decision. It is the same way with me and America."

He was born and reared in Nigeria. In 1999, as a young priest, he went to Rome to complete a master's degree in theology and to work on a doctorate. He was sent to the United States in 2003 to work in a parish and write his dissertation. His first stop was Lake Havasu.

"But over time I saw that my ministry might not be in a parish but in a place like a hospital," Father Fidelis told me. "I love people. That is what led me to become a priest. And that is what led me to become a chaplain in a hospital."

He was certified in what is called "clinical pastoral education" and now works as a chaplain at Banner Good Samaritan Medical Center in Phoenix. "It can be very difficult, but I love it," he told me. "I like the diversity of the people. I learn from them, how they deal with disease and mortality. And I wish to help them. I have found that when a person is sick, the whole family is sick, so we work very hard to take care of all of them. That is very challenging, but I enjoy it so much."

He has been going through the citizenship process for eight years. He finally was sworn in at a ceremony earlier this month.

"I cried when we recited the Pledge of Allegiance," he told me. "I wish that my Mother could have seen that. (She passed away some months ago.) She taught me to dream big dreams. And in some ways, there is no bigger dream than to be a citizen here. It was not only me who felt this way. I could see it in all of the others who were made citizens that day. It was beautiful."

Now that he is one of us, I asked Father Fidelis what he was looking forward to most as a full-fledged citizen.

"I cannot wait to exercise my right to vote," he said. "And I would like someday to receive a request for jury duty."

Natural-born Americans often skip that first thing and try to get out of the second, I told him.

"To know that I can now participate and contribute, that is a wonderful thing to me," he said. "Even a little overwhelming. I cannot wait."

See what I mean? There are times when it takes a newly minted American to remind the rest of us how good we have it.

"What a gift it is for me to have the job that I have," he said. "to minister to people who are in need. To pray with them. Be there for them. And also to know that now I am a citizen. After all these gifts, what I want most is only to participate and to be of service."

Patriotism can be corny and uncool. But for meeting someone like Father Fidelis, it's hard not to believe that sentimental old Irving Berlin was on to something. God really does bless America.[247]

---

247   E.J. Montini, *Arizona Republic* columnist, published, July 17, 2011

Appendix II

Nigerian priest called to serve in America

Fidelis Igwenwanne had a vision when he was a young boy growing up in Nigeria. As time went on, it became clear that he was called to serve God. Today, Igwenwanne is a priest at Lake Havasu City's Our Lady of the Lake Roman Catholic Church.

The parish has more than 2,500 families, and much of Igwenwanne's day is spent tending to their spiritual needs.

He consults with couples who are preparing for marriage, makes daily hospital calls, and hears confessions at least once a week.

But his favorite part of being a priest is celebrating the Holy Eucharist. The Eucharist is a circular wafer that a priest gives to parishioners at the end of Mass. Catholics believe it is the body of Christ. By offering the Eucharist, "You are leading (people) to Christ," Igwenwanne said.

The most intriguing part of his ministry, he said, is consoling the terminally ill. Igwenwanne reminds the sick that Christ also suffered. "Sickness and suffering—they should be viewed in the context of Christ's suffering," he said. "Jesus triumphed from suffering. So that is why I stay close to them-to give them focus so that they will know that Christ will be the solver of their problems. Priests are called to lead people to God. I feel called to the job I am in, and I love the job I am in."

Igwenwanne has been a priest for 16 years. He began his ministry in Nigeria's Issele-Uku diocese. From there, he went to Rome, where he studied at Pontifical Urban University. At the time he was trying to figure out where God wanted him to serve.

During a break in studying, he visited friends in Phoenix. He fell in love with the city and decided to continue his ministry there. Three years ago, the Phoenix diocese assigned him to Our Lady of the Lake. "I love it here. I'm thrilled to be here. It's a nice place to be," he said.

Igwenwanne spends much of his spare time preparing homilies. He also enjoys writing. Mostly, he writes about religion. He has written three books-Come Holy Spirit, God the Father of Love, and A Priest Who is He Amongst You-and is working on a fourth.

Igwenwanne also is a man of many tongues. He is fluent in English, Italian and Igbo (a Nigerian dialect. He can read and write Latin, and is learning Spanish. He said he dreams in English interspersed with Igbo. On occasion, an Italian phrase will find its way into his sleep, he said.

Many people do not know that Igwenwanne is very sociable. He loves to sing and dance and has an eclectic taste in music. "I love to sit with different people and make lots of friends," he said. "I love people. I really do."[248]

---

248   Today's *News-Herald* Lake Havasu, October 13, 2006. You may reach the reporter at raap@havasunews.com

Selected Bibliography

Church Documents

Congregation for Clergy, Directory on the Ministry and life of Priests, Vatican City: Editrice Vaticana, 1994: AAS 87 (1995) 191-280.

John Paul II, Redemptor Hominis, Encyclical letter, 4th March, 1979: AAS 71 (1979) 257-324.

........., Pastores Dabo Vobis, Encyclical letter, 20th October, 1992: AAS 85 (1993) 234-298.

........., Familiaris Consortio, Apostolic Exhortation, 22 November, 1982; AAS 74, (1982), 81-190.

........., Christifideles Laici, Apostolic Exhortation, 30th December 988: AAS 81 (1989) 393-521

........., Redemptoris Missio, Encyclical letter on the Permanent Validity of the Missionary Mandate, 7 December, 1990: AAS 83 (1991) 249-340.

PAUL VI, Evangelii Nuntiandi, Apostolic Exhortation, 8 December, 1975: AAS 68 (1976) 5-76.

Vatican II, Lumen Gentium, Dogmatic Constitution on the Church 21 November, 1964: AAS 57 (1965) 5-75.

........., Decree on the Apostolate of Laity, Apostolicam Actuositatem,November 18 1965:AAS 58, 11 (1966), pp. 837-864.

........., Presbyterium Ordinis, Decree on the Ministry and Life of Priests, December 7, 1965:AAS 59, (1966) 865-912.

........., The Celebration of the Catholic Church, Liberia Editrice Vaticana, 1994

OTHER SOURCES

Dulles A, "Priest and Eucharist: No Higher Calling." in S.J. Rossetti, (ed) Born of the Eucharist: A Spirituality for Priests, Ave Maria Press, Notre Dame, 2009, 11-25.

Forrest, Tom, Ed. A Call to Holiness, London: Redemptoris Press, 1990.

Forrest, Tom, New Evangelization 2000, Vol. 23, 1994, p5-45

Gbuji, A.O. New Evangelization in Nigeria Ten Years After the Pope's Visit, Onitsha: Veritas Press, 1992.

Okoye, G.M.P. Priestly Life, Enugu: Akam Press, 1977.

Powell, John. He Touched Me, Dublin: Gold Press, Dublin, 1978.

Rossetti, Stephen, Born of the Eucharist: A Spirituality for Priests, Ave Maria Press, Notre Dame: 2009

Rossetti, S.J. "The Eucharist: A Call to Priestly Holiness," in S.J. Rossetti (ed) Born of the Eucharist: A Spirituality for Priests, 80-95.

_____. The Joy of the Priests, Ave Maria Press, Notre Dame 2005

William, Ryan D. The Other Christ, New York: Shed and Ward Press, 1961.

ABOUT THE BOOK

Do not expect to read this book as you might read most other books. It is designed to give more than mere information. It offers the reader a broader understanding and deeper appreciation of the nature of the priesthood and the personality of priest, especially his duality, (an ordinary man and man of God) amidst God's people, as he operates within them and in whom they deal with daily. It is calculated to enlarge the reader's view of the priests' behavior and this will strengthen their ability to love, deal closely and more realistically with him, (the priest). This book tries to help the reader get the most out of experience of a priest. In fact, it is a guide to greater peace of mind and increased spiritual vitality.

Its ultimate goal is a more satisfying and a more enlightened and grace filled relationship to priests throughout your life which will ultimately lead you to God in the life to come. To absorb its rich message into your being, will require time, reflection, application, and persevering practice.

"It is good you get this book so as to learn the relevant ways of acquiring holiness of life that will bring joy, blessing, self-fulfilment and unity with God. I recommend the book to priests, seminarians, lay men and women looking for sound and up to the moment spiritual book.

Have one here with Fr. Fidelis has put right into your hands by his publication of this book. *A Man for God and for Others*, and recommend it to friends and others.